Parents Assuring Student Success

Achievement Made Easy by Learning Together

Second Edition

John R. Ban

national educational service

Copyright © 2000 by National Educational Service
304 West Kirkwood Avenue
Bloomington, Indiana 47404
(800) 733-6786 (toll free) / (812) 336-7700
FAX: (812) 336-7790

Cover design by Grannan Graphic Design Ltd.
Text design and composition by T.G. Design Group

Printed in the United States of America

ISBN 1-879639-72-6

TABLE OF CONTENTS

Foreword vii

Preface to Second Edition ix

History of PASS xi

Introduction 1

    The First Teacher, The First Classroom
    A Priority Plan for Parents in Need of Special Attention
    The PASS Curriculum
    The Importance of Studying and Learning
    Study Tips for Parents
    Learning and Fun

Workshop/Module 1: Parent Attitude 17

    Learning Begins in the Home
    Parents: The Critical Link
    Study More, Study Better
    A Weekly 20-Point Parent Checkup
    Parent Contract

Workshop/Module 2: The Home Environment 35

    Become a Learning Architect
    Know Your Child's Learning and Study Habits
    Frank Talk About Television
    TV Viewing Log

Workshop/Module 3: Study Skills (COLT) 47

    What Is Concentration?
    What Causes Concentration Problems?
    What Can Parents Do to Remove Distractions?
    Review of Concentration
    Listening Skills

Five Parent Rules on Listening
10-Point Listening Habits Checklist
Review of Listening
Time Management
Weekly Planning Log
Review of Time Management

Workshop/Module 4: Homework and Learning Expediters 65

Road to School Success
Homework Log
A Parent Primer on Homework
Homework Encounters
Common Homework Irritants
Learning Expediters (Teachers, Textbooks, Students, Computers)
The SSR Approach: Searching for Main Ideas
Review of Learning Expediters

Workshop/Module 5: Note-Taking Skills 87

Five Parent Guidelines
Note-Taking Designs
Outlining
Mapping
Review and Discussion for Parents

Workshop/Module 6: Preparing for Tests 99

The Pros and Cons of Taking Tests
Preparing for Tests
Taking Tests
Parents as Test Engineers
Kinds of Tests
Test-Makers
Parent Assistance: Preparing for Tests

Workshop/Module 7: Memory and Thinking Skills 109

What Parents Need to Know About Memory
Strategies for Memory Enhancement
Thinking and Problem Solving
Thinking Skills
Problem-Solving Skills
The PMI Method
Teaching Analogies
Teaching Synonyms and Antonyms
Review

Workshop/Module 8: Reading Skills 125
 The Nature of Reading
 Three Interventions to Facilitate Reading
 Student Comparison Notebook
 Comprehension Notebook Form
 Know Your Child's Reading and Study Habits
 Reading Speed
 Silent Versus Oral Reading
 Motivating Children to Read
 Parent-Child Word Activities

A Final Word 143

Evaluation Form 149

About the Author 153

FOREWORD

There is no higher calling in America than the education of its children. The reason is plain. Children will determine what our country is going to be like in years ahead. They will decide its citizens' quality of life. Seeing to it that they can read, write, and solve problems intelligently is not just the duty of schools. It is the duty of everyone. Above all, it is the duty of the child's primary caretakers—his or her parents. The drumbeat for parent involvement in a child's learning grows stronger every day. It has turned the nation's attention and taken on a sense of urgency.

This manual is about parents and their educational responsibilities. While there are many books offering parents advice on how to function as teachers in the home, this book presents a different twist. It lays out an easy-to-follow, systematic method for doing this. Its strength lies in its simplicity, organization, and energy. In sum, this is a family self-help manual. It is a clarion call for families to immerse themselves in their children's learning. Most importantly, it shows them how.

Dr. Ban has pulled from the mosaic of ideas on study skills those that can be easily taught to parents for home application. He has used these ideas with parents in several urban school systems. His blueprint for an expanded parent role in the classroom is simple: train parents in study skills to help improve their own children's study skills.

The strongest message of the book is that parents do make a difference. Dr. Ban has done a masterful job of making this point. The need for parental involvement today is critical because everything we now know about teaching and learning indicates that the parent is the first teacher. This is especially true at a time when we are observing the dissolution of the family structure. The future looks bleak if we cannot get the parent back into the teaching/learning equation.

I endorse this book because I plan to use it as a handbook for working not only with families in need of extra help, but with families that may need extra help in the future. Dr. Ban has put together the best resource I have seen in the literature on what parents can do to help their children succeed.

—Dr. Norman D. Comer
Former Superintendent of Schools
School City of East Chicago
East Chicago, Indiana

PREFACE TO SECOND EDITION

This second edition of *Parents Assuring Student Success* (PASS) includes new material to enrich the text and give parents an even deeper insight into their role as "home teachers." The goal of this edition, like that of the first edition, is to give parents a strong information base and show them how to use a wide variety of strategies to improve their child's study skills.

While some study skills are time-tested, needing little or no changes, others require refinement because of advances in research and technology. This second edition includes more parent interactive exercises, fresh advice from parents and teachers, and a section on computers. This section is included because we can no longer separate study skills from technological advances in today's world. Clearly, computers have assumed a powerful relationship with learning.

Many parents have benefited from the lessons of the first edition of PASS. In any self-help book, not all recommendations work for everyone. There will be unexpected roadblocks to applying well-meaning advice at home. Experts are not the only ones with good ideas. Parents themselves may invent exercises that work best for their children. That is why this workbook urges parents to experiment, trying different practices and customizing them to meet the needs of their children.

No one publication on parenting will have all of the answers. Consequently, parents should not become discouraged if certain practices in the workbook do not work when first applied at home. Keep your hands on the wheel; you may see results over time. Moreover, talk to other parents to find out what they did or what worked for them in tapping their children's study potential. There is much to gain from the wisdom of other parents. Also, weave together what you hear from teachers, ministers, youth service workers, and family-life specialists as you prepare to become study skill learners yourselves. Don't give up! Make this your battle cry.

Each chapter in this edition is organized around a simple format that is easy to follow. PASS continues to focus on parents working diligently with their children to develop study skills that are essential to learning.

A new addition is the brief evaluation form at the end of the workbook. By having a chance to evaluate the program, parents can reach their own conclusions on how well the workbook has served them. Together, parents can work as a group to evaluate workshop topics. Group work can be a valuable learning experience for all parents. Or parents can fill out the evaluation by themselves. Parent workshop leaders are not bound by the evaluation form. They are free to design and use their own.

HISTORY OF PASS

PASS stands for Parents Assuring Student Success. The word itself means an opening or road through rough terrain, marking the way to a certain destination. PASS shows parents the passageway to improving their children's education.

PASS resulted from three years of discussion with parents and educators. It was used in an urban school system in Northwest Indiana with a large number of families who were in need of extra help. This district had an abiding belief in the value of parent education and was willing to commit resources to a program that addresses the source, not just the symptoms, of poor student learning in school—the home.

I approached the school superintendent about working with families in his district, training them to teach their children study skills. He arranged a meeting with elementary principals and central office administrators to examine PASS. After considerable discussion, they enthusiastically backed this program.

The next step was the presentation of PASS to a diverse parent review group brought together by the school administration. Throughout the winter and spring, this parent group studied and reviewed PASS. With their endorsement, the members of this Parent PASS Committee developed many details of the program: publicity; selection of workshop sites, times, and days; parent attendance; transportation; baby-sitting; hospitality; and budget.

When planning was completed, PASS was submitted to the district school board, which unanimously gave its blessing to the program.

From the very beginning, PASS was molded by parents. The administration generously supplied resources and encouragement for this parent education project. A central office administrator was designated as liaison between school and parents, and served as a valuable facilitator, ensuring that everything ran smoothly. It was the parents, however, who were the bulwark of the program. They did the leg work, planning, monitoring, and attending to parent needs. They maintained substantial ownership of the program. Their love for children was the driving force behind their labors.

I designed the curriculum for PASS, rallied parent planning, and was the instructor for the workshops scheduled in two-week intervals. Many ideas for this program were chipped from the mountain of advice built by experts on study skills. To all of them, a debt of gratitude is owed.

The effort to increase parental participation in classroom learning proved successful. This finding was based on an evaluation of parent responses to the study skills learned at the workshops and later practiced in the home. The most noticeable impact of PASS was the change in parent attitude. Clearly evident was the unshakable resolve of many parents to take greater responsibility for their children's learning. This is precisely what is needed to ignite a fire for change. I hope that such a blaze will spread swiftly along the parched landscape of American education.

—John R. Ban

INTRODUCTION

THE FIRST TEACHER, THE FIRST CLASSROOM

The clamor to have our students do better in school rises with each passing day. Who should take the lead in ensuring that this happens is the key question facing this country. Some say the federal government; others point to individual states. Still others insist that this is the school's job. The fact is it is everybody's job—especially those in the home.

Education is our nation's most enduring treasure. This is why everyone wants it to work. Given this, the public is outraged at the lack of learning on the part of thousands of students. Virtually everyone has an idea on how to fix this problem. For instance, there have been massive infusions of money. The federal government's Title I program alone has poured 118 billion dollars into poor neighborhood schools over the past two decades. Still, children there continue to underachieve.

On the state level, lawmakers have tried to jump-start local schools in a variety of ways. Since 1999, all states, except Nebraska and Iowa, have mandated statewide assessment of student progress. This extensive testing operation is intended to measure how much children are learning in school. To the dismay of many, the failure rate on these tests remains high.

Failure in school can be linked to failure in the home. Parents are often busier with their own lives than with their children's. Student underachievement is often the result of parents not doing their job. If all parents did their best to help their children develop skills to succeed in school, the problem of below-average student performance would vanish.

If the bad news in our country is that students are not learning enough, the good news is that the home is the switch for converting student failure into student success. It starts with parents asking two questions: "What's happening in my child's school?" and "Is there something I can do to assist teachers with the enormous job of educating my child?"

The answer to these questions follows.

This manual provides a stairway to greater family involvement in a child's education. It tries to draw home and school, parent and child, closer together. This is the "connection" that almost everyone believes will lead to improved student performance in the classroom.

Parents are a child's first teacher, and the home is a child's first classroom. While school is an important part of a child's world, children spend less than one-third of their lives there. The influence of the school is, therefore, limited. Not so for the home. As a child's main nesting place, its influence stretches far. Parents have the greatest impact on children during their formative years, when study habits and attitudes take shape.

Most family life experts contend that the best way to teach children a love for learning while they are growing up is for their parents to become learners, too. Parents must strive to instill in their children the thrill of learning about the world, themselves, and others. Self-discovery is a powerful educational tool.

Since parents are in charge where learning begins, they are in the best position to motivate their children to succeed in school. Clearly, parents are the key to upgrading education throughout America by lending teachers a helping hand.

An effective way for parents to help teachers increase student achievement is by becoming learning facilitators. This does not mean that they have to become experts in reading, mathematics, science, or social studies to help their children acquire higher grades in school. It does mean that they have to learn some basic techniques for improving their children's study habits. These are techniques that all parents can learn. They require neither special preparation nor a long period of training.

Most parents want to help their children do better in school. The problem is that they do not know how. They lack the skills and knowledge to help out. To correct this, parents must not only assume the role of "home teacher," they must also have some training to prepare for this role. This manual provides such a training program.

PASS is about collaboration; it draws on the talents and energies of parents to assist educators in raising educational standards for every child. Its overriding theme is the centrality of the home in raising student achievement. This theme is in keeping with the national trend to deepen home involvement in all phases of a child's learning and to make parents the axis of the school reform movement.

In raising children, there is frequent talk about "teachable moments." These are times when children are most receptive to learning. Teachers know about this. So should parents. Parents need to set aside time for these teachable moments in their daily schedule as their children grow up. This will enable them to enter their children's world; to stay in touch with their children; to talk more to them, and preach less; to teach them lessons about being a good student; and to show them that you truly care about them. All these will dramatically increase the odds that children will get good grades in school.

When do these teachable moments occur? They occur nearly all of the time. Parents need only gain access to their children's world and stay there, especially as they journey through school. As parents learn more about study skills, they can teach these skills to their children in teachable moments on car rides, at dinner time, while watching television together, at weekly family meetings, when children ask questions, or when they are relaxed or troubled. What to teach them at these precious times is what this manual is all about.

This manual consists of two major parts. The first part teaches parents what it takes to become an efficient learner. Here, the focus is on study skills, including the principles and characteristics of well-known learning strategies. Such strategies are associated with successful achievement in school.

The second part of this manual gives parents the opportunity to acquire skills in teaching and reinforcing critical study habits at home. These are skills people can easily learn, either by themselves or with others. Furthermore, these skills can be practiced with children in the familiar surroundings of the home.

Study skills need to be taught to children when they are young, because what we do early with children affects them later in school. Knowing how to study will give children the ability to succeed in school and help them feel good about themselves. Study skills discipline students for learning. When students become more disciplined learners, their schoolwork will show improvement throughout their formative years.

Normally, study skills refer to reading, writing, homework, time management, taking notes, and the like. They are study habits that make learning easier for the child. One study skills expert, Herman Ohme, defines study skills as efficient ways for using your time and mind.

The goal of study skills is to produce an independent learner, one who can learn on his or her own and perform well in and out of school. Study skills are building blocks of success, and that is why they are important to every child.

While teachers are normally expected to teach study skills to students, few actually do. The reasons are the lack of time, the large number of students in classes, a preoccupation with covering subject matter, and the fact that most teachers were not trained in teaching study skills. Consequently, some teachers fail to give individual attention to students who lack good study habits. Parents are not usually involved in teaching study skills. They tend to be spectators in these matters. The majority of parents sit on the sidelines, content to leave their children's education to teachers. However, this view is changing with the increased recognition of the educational potential of the home. More is being demanded of parents.

The time has come to shift attention to the role of parents in the discussion on improving instruction. At the very least, parents should be involved in teaching their children how to learn. There is no more powerful way to improve American education.

The Parents Assuring Student Success program shows how to capitalize on the energy of parents to assist teachers in bolstering learning at home. PASS is a long-term, parent-friendly, skill development program. Its main purpose is to train parents to work with their children at home to instill those general study skills that are universally recognized as being linked to school success. Effective study skills raise student performance in language arts, science, mathematics, social studies, and other academic fields. Once schooled at home in specific techniques for learning, children should perform at a higher level in the classroom. Test scores should rise; so should students' motivation and self-esteem.

The specific objectives of PASS are to develop parent understanding of and skill in

❖ enhancing attitude

❖ providing a productive learning environment at home

❖ teaching children how to manage their time, listen to instruction, and concentrate in class

❖ managing homework and studying a textbook

❖ guiding children to prepare for and take tests

❖ taking notes and organizing information

❖ enhancing memory and thinking processes

❖ teaching reading at home

These understandings and skills will be covered in the following modules. Parents can study these modules on their own or meet in workshop sessions conducted by the PTA, block clubs, church groups, service organizations, school administrators, Head Start programs, Chapter 1 affiliates, and other parent education programs.

There are advantages in bringing parents together in a workshop setting. They can learn from each other. Bonding and fellowship grow out of social learning. Furthermore, group study can be a source of support and reinforcement. Parents can share their experience with each other, reflecting on what works and what does not. Skills learned from each module of PASS can be applied at home.

This manual grew out of several considerations. First, there is an abundance of materials on study skills. Most of the materials are written for students and teachers; few are designed for parents, especially parents from disadvantaged backgrounds. There is even less material offering parents the choice of independent study or group work in learning how to teach their children study skills.

In addition, while many schools have study skills centers where students can get special help, many students find these places uninviting. Some students fear that if they go to the center, they will be considered special education students or labeled as slow learners. Their homes project no such stigma. Children tend to feel more comfortable in the familiar surroundings of home.

Parents can become a mighty force in school reform. They need only to transform their home into a study skills center, "staffed" by parents trained to help their children acquire effective study habits. Such assistance will make the teacher's job easier.

PASS gives parents more responsibility in their child's learning than they may be used to. It shows parents how to make the home not only a living place but also a learning place, and it recasts parents as facilitators of learning.

Most of all, this manual is meant to be worked with. It includes many exercises for parents in skill development. Parents are given frequent opportunities for reflection before and after interacting with the material. In addition, each module is introduced by a "Parent Study Guide." This introductory page gives an overview of what parents will learn and sets the stage for the module ahead.

There is repetition of some content throughout the modules. It is deliberate. The purpose is to reinforce important ideas in order to deepen understanding and quicken skill development.

This manual outlines a plan for the school and home to work together in sharpening a child's study habits. In a sense, it offers a crash course for parents. Throughout, parents are challenged to examine their parenting practices. They are also shown how they can make a difference in their children's performance in the classroom. What they learn from this manual will help them become closer to their children. Most important, it will enable them to assume a decided presence in their children's education.

In the end, this manual is a call for the empowerment of parents. It summons parents to use their vast potential in developing their children's brain power. With a step-by-step approach, the manual shows parents how to flex their educational muscles.

The great tragedy in American education is that countless parents utilize only a fraction of their talents and time overseeing their children's schoolwork. Such negligence results in a monumental waste of brain power in our country. To do better in school, what children need most from parents is time. Responding to that need, parents must develop their talents to use that time in advancing their children's learning. PASS addresses both issues.

A PRIORITY PLAN FOR PARENTS IN NEED OF SPECIAL ATTENTION

The PASS program has a special emphasis. Although it can be used with all parents, it specifically targets parents in need of extra help in urban areas. This is because student underachievement is particularly stubborn there. If parent training programs are to have any significant effect on classroom instruction in the most needy areas of the country, these families deserve special attention. They should be number one on education's priority list. The troubling fact is they are not.

One-third of the nation's young children are at risk of failing in school. Some children are at risk before they reach kindergarten. In virtually every community, there are families with children whose school work falls short of their capabilities. These families are at risk of having their children fail their subjects, waste class time, be held back one or two grades, misbehave, or drop out of school. Their energy for learning is low; their desire to attend school is even lower. Since these children are not making full use of their talents, they quickly fall behind other children. As expected, schoolwork becomes a source of frustration for them.

These families and their children require personalized attention. To guarantee this, many initiatives directed solely at this group need to be undertaken. PASS is just one initiative. Its objective is to recruit these parents in the war to improve their children's learning. In short, it is a blueprint for a massive self-help program for families in need of extra help.

Over the past decade, a growing circle of political and educational leaders has scripted a set of national goals for education. Heading the list is the goal that all children should be ready to learn when they begin school. One way to accomplish this goal is for all parents to learn how to teach their children effective study behaviors—the sooner, the better. Parents can best learn these skills by attending parent education programs set up for this purpose.

Clearly, these parents stand to gain the most from being taught study skills techniques to use with their children. Motivating them to learn these skills involves using strategies that they help formulate and tune to their special circumstances.

Here is a plan for these strategies. It has a dual purpose: to draw these parents into a parent training program focusing on improving their children's study skills and to supply them with incentives to attend all the training sessions. Called the PINSA plan (for Parents in Need of Special Attention), it consists of four strategies.

Strategy 1. PASS should be offered in a series of parent workshops geared to their neighborhoods.

Parents who are in need of extra help learn best in group settings. They tend to feel more comfortable studying with their peers. Group meetings can be designed as social outings as well as learning sessions, with "Fun and Learning—Together" as the drawing card. Moreover, these study skills workshops should be organized around the daily schedule of parents in their own neighborhood.

Strategy 2. PASS workshops should be planned by a parent team.

School principals, ministers, or social agency heads can identify parents with leadership ability to make up the parent planning team. A meeting of these parents can be called to explain the PASS program. This core group of parents should help plan, operate, and evaluate workshops.

PASS should be run by parents. Parent leaders should have ownership of the program. They can organize it around a single school in walking distance for all parents, not in a central spot miles away. The parent planning team could be broken into the following organizational committees:

Hospitality—provide music, door prizes, drinks, and snacks.

Publicity—spread the word about the program and notify parents of every single workshop.

Child Care—supply comprehensive child-care services.

Transportation —provide transportation to and from workshops.

Telephone—contact and work closely with parents who need extra help (see below).

Budget — plan the cost of these programs and secure funds to underwrite this cost.

Strategy 3. Workshops should include social activities as well as learning activities.

Parents are more motivated to participate in learning programs that provide fun, fellowship, and entertainment. All workshops should mix social activities with learning.

The hospitality committee has the job of creating a festive mood for the workshops. It should provide music, snacks, and greetings. Baby-sitting should also be made available. Emphasis should be placed by the publicity committee on the fun part of the program—a good time for all. Door prizes can whip up interest; music can help create a festive atmosphere. Parent learning activities should result in material that can be taken home and shared with children (headbands, book markers, folders, activity sheets, etc.).

Strategy 4. Organizers should target parents who need extra help and grant them preferential treatment in recruiting them to attend workshops.

Apathy among parents of children in need of extra help runs high. It is often difficult to get them to training sessions. These parents need special help because they are most in need of skills to help their children succeed in school. A campaign to draw them to workshops merits ongoing attention.

A special committee of parents (a PINSA committee) can assume responsibility for designing an aggressive plan to reach out to these parents. To start, this committee can compose a letter (see Sample A) to be mailed to these parents with the signature of the school superintendent. His signature will add a sense of importance to the program. This letter should also include a schedule of workshops (see Sample B).

Prior to each parent workshop, these parents could also be sent a reminder letter (see Sample C) that has been signed by the building principal.

Finally, a parent telephone committee should make personal calls to those parents identified by school administrators as parents who could benefit the most from the workshops. These parents should be placed on a select, preferential treatment list and politely called before every workshop. A parent escort might be needed to pick them up and accompany them to workshops.

Steps should be taken to provide child-care services for workshop participants. It is important to make it easy for young mothers and fathers to attend workshops by giving them the opportunity to leave their child in capable hands at the workshop site. Child-care should be more than custodial. It should be educational. People supervising the children should be experienced in providing growth and enhancement activities for children of different ages. Children should be involved in games and crafts. What they make can be displayed for the parents attending the workshops or put on exhibit at school board meetings.

If necessary, transportation to workshop sites should be arranged for these parents. Carpooling can promote a feeling of togetherness. Notes of thanks and appreciation should be written by the parent committee charged with recruiting these parents for the workshops. In addition, door prizes and awards for attendance can be used as lures for these parents. Other incentives for attendance should be explored by this parent committee.

SAMPLE A

Dear _____,

     Please accept this letter as a personal invitation to attend a series of parent workshops offered by the _____ School District. The first one will be on Thursday, September 19, 20___, at the Education Center on Lake Road. It will start at 6:00 p.m. and end at 8:30 p.m. There will be refreshments, music, prizes, and a good time for all.

     Your child needs your help to succeed in school. You are the most important person in your child's life. You can make a difference in how well your child does in school. These workshops will show you how.

     All the workshops will focus on seven study skills you can teach your child at home. You will learn simple ways to teach these study skills. From your efforts at home, your child's study habits will improve, and so should grades and test scores.

     There will be child-care services at the workshops. Feel free to bring your young children with you. They will be supervised by experienced child-care personnel. If you need a ride to the workshops, contact your school's principal or PTO officers.

     Please show your love for your children by attending these workshops. They are depending on you. See you on the 19th.

     Sincerely,

SAMPLE B

Parent Workshop Schedule
Education Center, Lake Side Schools

Workshop 1: Attitude
Topic: Developing an Attitude That Encourages Student Learning
Thursday, September 5, 20_____   6:00–8:30 p.m.

Workshop 2: The Home Environment
Topic: Turning the Home Into a Learning Place
Thursday, September 19, 20_____   6:00–8:30 p.m.

Workshop 3: Study Skills
Topic: Improving Your Child's Concentration Skills, Listening Skills,
           and Time-Management Skills
Thursday, October 3, 20_____   6:00–8:30 p.m.

Workshop 4: Homework and Learning Expediters
Topic: Helping Children With Homework and Understanding Their Textbooks
Thursday, October 17, 20_____   6:00–8:30 p.m.

Workshop 5: Note-Taking Skills
Topic: Helping Children Take Notes and Organize Information
Thursday, October 24, 20_____   6:00–8:30 p.m.

Workshop 6: Preparing for Tests
Topic: Helping Children Prepare for and Take Examinations
Thursday, November 7, 20_____   6:00–8:30 p.m.

Workshop 7: Memory and Thinking Skills
Topic: Developing Your Child's Thinking and Memory Skills
Thursday, November 21, 20_____   6:00–8:30 p.m.

Workshop 8: Reading Skills
Topic: Helping Your Child Become a Better Reader
Thursday, December 5, 20_____   6:00–8:30 p.m.

SAMPLE C

Dear _____ ,

I personally invite you to become part of a series of exciting parent education workshops offered by the _____ School District. The next one will be given on October 3 at 6:00 p.m. in the Education Service Center on Lake Road.

The workshops are designed to help you become involved in improving your child's study habits at home. You will learn seven study skills that are simple ways to guide your student to better grades and test scores. This is an excellent opportunity to share in your child's education.

We don't want you to miss out on this experience. All the workshops are held on Thursday evening from 6:00 p.m. to 8:30 p.m. A schedule of workshops is enclosed. You should have a great time there! There are refreshments, prizes, music, and supervised child care for your younger children. Need a ride? Just contact your school's principal or PTO office, and they will arrange transportation for you.

Your child is counting on you. You can make a difference. I hope to see you at the workshops.

Sincerely,

THE PASS CURRICULUM

Central to the success of PASS is its curriculum. It consists of seven study skills that can be learned or taught in any order. One skill is not dependent on another.

As indicated earlier, this program is arranged in a modular, workshop format so it can be studied by groups of parents. Since the topics are not sequential, parents who miss a workshop are not at a disadvantage when they attend another. If parents want to study this program on their own, the present arrangement allows them to do so.

Whatever the learning format, parents need to warm up before plunging into the units. They can do this by inspecting the condensed program below. This snapshot of PASS enables parents to quickly review the program's major parts and how they fit together.

Become a "Home Teacher"

There are three steps to becoming a "home teacher" or learning facilitator. The first is to develop an attitude that you can make your child a winner in school. The second is to redesign your home as a learning center. The third step is to spend time in acquiring specific skills for helping your child learn. These steps are outlined below.

Step 1: Develop a positive attitude.

1. Believe that you are important as a teacher and parent.

2. Believe that you can make a difference in your child's doing his or her best in school.

3. Believe that you can learn the skills to become a learning facilitator.

Step 2: Create a home learning environment that provides physical and emotional support.

1. Set aside a special study area (SSA) for your child.

2. Identify and highlight the SSA.

3. Equip and supply the SSA.

4. Label storage facilities and supplies in the SSA.

5. Model behavior and attitude about the importance of schoolwork.

   a. Use your leisure time for playing or talking with your child.

   b. Read where your child can see you.

   c. Talk about school, learning, and education.

   d. Watch TV programs on education and learning.

   e. Review closely all information sent home by schools.

6. Reinforce good study habits.

    a. Use words and compliments to build your child's self-esteem.

    b. Write upbeat notes and "mail" them to your child.

    c. Do something special for your child when he or she does well in school.

    d. Display your child's schoolwork in the home.

    e. Show respect for the power of learning and the world of ideas.

Step 3: Acquire specific skills for assisting learning in the home. Becoming competent in study skills requires hard work and practice. More specifically, it requires learning how to

1. Help your child manage study time.

2. Help your child do homework.

3. Help your child read better.

4. Help your child understand how to use textbooks and prepare for tests.

5. Help your child become an active listener in school and improve his or her concentration.

6. Strengthen your child's memory and thinking powers.

7. Help your child learn to organize information and take notes.

Study skills are learning tools; they are devices for using one's study time efficiently. Most of all, they give children the power to learn in school, to be successful there, and to feel better about themselves as learners.

Children will not get the most out of their education unless they know how to study. Good study habits will help children through the rough spots not only in school but also throughout their lives. These skills spell the difference between a good future and a bad one. Learning skills stay with a person for a lifetime. Carl Rogers hit it on the head when he remarked that the "only man who is educated is the man who has learned to learn."

THE IMPORTANCE OF STUDYING AND LEARNING

There are two major reasons why children do well in school: either they have the interest, desire, or drive to do well or they possess skills to study and learn. Conversely, the two major reasons why children do not do well in school are either that they do not have the motivation or they do not have the study skills necessary for succeeding in school.

Studying is an important activity in a person's life. It is through studying that people learn, whether the studying is by reading, writing, listening, or asking questions. Studying invigorates the mind. In importance, it ranks with eating, relaxing, sleeping, playing, and other functions of living.

Learning starts at birth and continues through life. One learns in and out of school. Learning leads to an education that no one can take away. An education liberates people. It offers them choices. Without choices, life is a one-way street that leads to nowhere. Education is a roadway to somewhere. For children, learning opens up a world of choices to improve their lives. Knowing how to study makes learning easier. Parents can help their children learn how to study by working closely with their children at home. The trick in helping your children succeed in school is to make learning useful and fun.

STUDY TIPS FOR PARENTS

Much is known about the dynamics of learning. Effective learning does not just happen. It is the result of hard work. Moreover, it takes time. Children learn by watching others, asking questions, doing things, making mistakes, reading, going to school, and especially by studying. Parents may not be able to control some ways in which children learn. They can, however, set aside time to learn how to cultivate their children's study habits in order to improve their learning in school. Below are seven tips to guide parents in their efforts to improve their children's study habits. As you work through this manual, return to these tips on occasion to refresh your memory of these important study considerations.

Tip 1: Practice

It takes practice to learn how to study. And practice takes time. Time needs to be set aside for a child to practice a study skill. Practice involves mental and physical effort. The more children practice a study skill, the better they will become at it.

Tip 2: Routine

Good students make it a habit to study; they build it into their daily lives. Studying is easier when it becomes a part of a child's routine. Students who do not study regularly at home seldom excel in school.

Tip 3: Environment

Studying is more effective when the physical environment supports mental work. A productive study site requires proper lighting, ventilation, temperature, furniture, solitude, and learning supplies. These conditions heighten the mood for learning.

Tip 4: Health

Studying and learning require a healthy mind and body. A child will be unable to handle the rigors of mental work if he or she is not in good health. Schoolwork demands good vision and hearing. It also requires proper rest, a healthy diet, and adequate exercise.

Tip 5: Attitude

Children will not apply themselves to schoolwork unless they believe it is important. Their attitude toward learning determines what kind of students they are going to be. The home attitude is a critical factor in a child's school attitude. Once children believe they can become successful students and receive this message from those around them, they will be more eager to practice those study skills that enable them to learn.

Tip 6: Encouragement and Support

A pat on the back, either for effort or performance, does wonders for children. It is a powerful motivator. Children learn more when they routinely receive encouragement from their parents. Psychologist Rudolf Dreikurs warns us that "children need encouragement like plants need water." Again, children will perform better in school when their parents support them in their studies.

Tip 7: Memory and Thinking

Learning is not only memorizing facts. It is also making sense out of those facts. It is drawing relationships, understanding principles, and finding meaning in what is studied. Studying any topic should always include both memorizing information and reflecting on that information.

LEARNING AND FUN

If learning involves so much time and energy, can it be fun, too? Absolutely! But it will never be fun unless children are good at it. Mental effort is difficult for many children. If they do not have the opportunity to exercise their mind at home, they will find it difficult to do so in school.

It bears repeating that practice produces good study habits. Once acquired, study habits ease the way to learning. When learning becomes easy for students, they will find it to be more enjoyable.

Parents have the power to show that studying and learning can be enjoyable. Studying will appeal to children once they see that it gets results. A parent's job is to help children develop skills in studying so that they can succeed in school.

Learning is a change in behavior. Children learn all the time as they grow up. Parents learn, too. They can learn how to help their children learn. It is not easy. But parents have to begin in the home. To break ground, parents can heed the following reminders:

❖ Be a learner yourself. Read and watch the news or current event shows. Talk frequently about ideas with friends and family. Children copy what they see their parents do.

❖ Always talk about the importance of learning with your children; talk, do not nag.

❖ Spend short periods of time working with your child on specific study skills; allow sufficient rest time in between.

❖ Remember that short study periods are more effective for young children than long ones.

❖ Sharpen learning through repetition and drills. A skill is best learned through practice. See to it that your child practices a study skill over and over.

❖ Do not do your children's work for them. Children learn more by doing things for themselves. Help them understand how to do their own work.

❖ Help children learn tough topics more easily by breaking the topics into smaller parts. These parts can be studied separately. Later on, time can be spent on studying how bits of information fit together.

❖ Identify each child's individual learning style. Not all children learn in the same way. Some learn best by seeing (visual learners); others, by hearing or listening (auditory learners). Still others learn best through touch (kinesthetic learners). Many children prefer to learn on their own. Others learn better in groups, studying with others. Some children like to learn while listening to music; others prefer a quiet environment. By spending time with their children while they learn at home, parents will gain insight into their major learning style.

Learning expert Robert E. Valett gives five rules for learning, which correspond to the letters of the word "learn." They serve as helpful guidelines for parents determined to be teachers at home.

Listen carefully.

Exert yourself.

Aspire to achievement.

Reason well.

Nurture your interests and talents.

All these rules are important. The most important one for parents is to exert themselves. This means taking action, making the effort, assuming personal responsibility to ensure that their children acquire effective study habits.

Let's get started by turning to the first module.

Parent Attitude

PARENT STUDY GUIDE 1

FOCUS　　　Forming a helping attitude regarding student learning

PURPOSE　　Developing an understanding of the role of attitude in becoming a learning facilitator

SKILL　　　Conditioning yourself to make a difference in your child's learning

REFLECTION　Sharing your thoughts, before and after this lesson, on the importance and role of attitude

Before:

After:

ATTITUDE

LEARNING BEGINS IN THE HOME

Welcome to this training program. It comes at a time when the picture of public education is grim, and educators are searching for ways to change the public cynicism toward the schools.

Many are unhappy with the schools. Calls for reform and radical change echo throughout the country. Politicians and others bemoan low test scores, poor student study habits, budget woes, fights over school choice, unmotivated students, violence in the schools, and parent apathy. Parents everywhere are asking: "What can be done about our school's sorry state? What is the answer?" One answer is found by looking into a mirror. Parents, themselves, can become the answer when they become involved.

The cry for the need to improve our schools traces far back in our history. The cry that parents are indispensable in bringing this about is a roar that has never been louder. The fact is that no one person can save the schools. It will take the efforts of many. The home is the place to begin, and parents are the key. In the final analysis, schools will be saved from the bottom (homes) not from the top (the bureaucracy). Results will flow more quickly from the work of front-line troops than from the plans of headquarter chiefs.

More than anything else, what parents do in the home will determine the quality of student work in school. Parents can spearhead the drive to raise the quality of education. PASS offers parents the training for such an initiative.

As a parent education program, PASS is based on four premises:

1. Improvement in education starts in the homes and neighborhoods of America. The sooner we make these true learning places, the sooner learning will improve in the schools.

2. Parents have the potential to become "learning facilitators," teachers at home. It is up to parents to give children the tools to do well in schools. It is the home's responsibility to get children ready for learning.

3. The surest way for parents to raise their children's level of achievement in school is to teach them school survival skills. These are more commonly referred to as study skills.

4.   All parents, regardless of their background and circumstances, can learn these study skills either through an intensive training program completed on their own or in concert with others.

PASS is based on the idea that learning is a collective enterprise, one that takes many hands to make it work. To paraphrase an African proverb: "It takes a whole village to educate a child." What that means is that schools cannot educate children by themselves. They need help from others, especially from those in the home.

PASS calls for a stronger partnership between parents and teachers. Children do not learn from teachers alone; they learn from parents, too. After all, the home is where education begins. Echoing throughout the halls of schools is an SOS from teachers. Desperately, teachers are pleading for parents to give them a hand. PASS shows how parents can come to the rescue.

PASS mobilizes parent power. This power is always more effective when parents have the skills to exercise it. In a short period of time, PASS gives parents the muscle to lift the motivational level of their children in school.

Throughout PASS, one major theme stands out. That is, teachers can do a better job teaching children if parents do their job by getting children ready to learn in school. To send children to school ready to learn requires two things from parents. First, they must make the effort to acquire skills in teaching their children effective study habits at home. Second, they must spend time with their children applying these skills.

The ideas in this manual are well-known. They are found in the many volumes written on study skills. Most of the literature on this subject has been designed for students or teachers. In recent years, however, a number of books on this topic have been directed at parents. This manual is for parents, too, particularly parents of children in need of extra help. It translates the large body of knowledge on study skills for parent interaction and arranges it in a format suitable for the parent learner.

PARENTS: THE CRITICAL LINK

The first step parents must take to help their children cultivate effective study habits is to fine-tune their own attitude. Attitude makes the difference in the success of any effort. It is the flame that lights the fire of effort.

Parents must be believers. They must believe that they can influence how well their children do in school. They must believe that the best way to help their children in school is by teaching them proper study habits. Parents must further believe that these study habits can be taught in the home. Finally, they must believe that if they persevere, their efforts will pay off in time. Disregard disappointments. Remember the advice of Thomas Edison: "Keep trying, for every setback or failure is a step forward."

A parent is what a parent believes. Smart parents believe in the value of education. Education is power. It enables your children to make a future for themselves. Education is obtained through learning. Every parent can empower his or her child to learn in school by becoming a learning facilitator at home.

Many parents think that they are unimportant in their children's education. They may feel that they have no clout, no influence, no authority to change things. They may think that only presidents, governors, champions, generals, scientists, or rich people can change the world. Parents are normally mired down in doing small, uneventful things. What they do, it is often felt, really does not matter. Nothing is further from the truth. Helen Keller could have been talking about parents when she once remarked that "the world is not only moved by the mighty shoves of heroes but also by the aggregate of the tiny pushes of each honest worker."

All parents are important. They have enormous responsibilities. This is so because they are in charge of raising children who will run our planet in the future. It is not difficult to understand that the world's harvest depends on the seeds parents sow. Think of what your children's lives would be like without you. You are special to them; you are the brightest star in their small constellation.

While parents do attend to small, routine things in life, this does not detract from their importance. Parents need only to heed the advice of the great humanitarian, Mother Teresa: "do small things with great love." Indeed, parents may view themselves as small hinges, but small hinges allow big doors to swing open. Like small hinges, parents have fantastic power in their children's world.

The 10 most paralyzing words for parents are: "No, I can't do it; I can't make a difference." Conversely, the 10 most inspirational words for parents are: "Yes, I can do it; I can make a difference." These 10 words mark the pathway to successful parenting.

Some time ago, the late Johnny Weissmuller, the actor who played Tarzan in the movies, was giving a pep talk to budding actors. He was asked for his advice to prepare them for their craft. He curtly replied that the best advice he could give is, "Don't let go of the vine." No better advice can be given to parents who are struggling to help their children do better in school. Hang on tight to your convictions; do not let go of your dream of wanting to make a difference in the lives of your children. Swing past those who say "I can't." Pound your chest and bellow: "I can! I will!"

If parents were asked if they love their children, most would surely reply, "Yes." But if they were asked to present evidence of this love, many would pause a long time. Some would then say that they provide food for their child. Others would declare that they give their children clothing and shelter. Still others would remark that they give their children an education as a sign of their love.

The law demands that parents provide those things for their children. Such generosity does not reflect any special love parents have for their children. On the other hand, if parents say that their evidence of love is shown in the time they spend with their children and the effort they make in preparing their child to succeed in life, that would be the most convincing proof of their love. Remember the saying: It's easy to become a parent; it takes a lot of work to become a mom or dad.

Your worth as a parent is measured not by how wealthy you are, how large your bank account, how many cars in your garage, how many friends you have, or how high your status in life. No, the yardstick of your worth as a parent and human being is how well you raise your children. This can be the truest gauge of anyone's success in life.

To raise children well today requires that you spend time with them and help them learn. As mentioned before, learning is power. Skill in learning is the best way for a child to prepare for the future and cope with life. Parents can give no more valuable gift to their children than good study skills. Study skills guarantee them a good education. A good education increases their chances for a good life.

Children, especially those from disadvantaged households, face a mountain of problems and pressures while growing up. Parents can help push this mountain aside. Following the lead of the inspirational speaker and talk show host Montel Williams, all they have to do is to teach their children the chant: "Mountain, get out of my way!" This line from the gospel song, "Move, Mountain, Move," demonstrates a determination that children can climb the ladder of success and overcome life's obstacles.

Children are what parents leave here on earth long after they are gone. They are a reflection of their parents. Furthermore, they display their parents' attitude toward education.

There are no seat belts for parents traveling the rocky roads of educating children. Bumps and bruises come with the terrain. Parents, however, have it within their power to smooth the journey in several ways. One is by becoming knowledgeable about study habits, children, and schoolwork. Another is by learning how to teach their children specific study skills. Still another way is by cultivating an attitude, a resolve, a conviction that you are going to be a decisive factor in your child's education.

Attitudes are mental pictures. People are driven by the mental pictures they create. These can be negative or positive pictures. All of us have the ability to create positive pictures, positive thoughts, of ourselves and what we can do. Positive attitudes make us feel good about ourselves. They give us confidence in our gift to be a force in our children's lives.

Your success as a parent is governed by your attitude. Having the right attitude will give you an edge; it will keep you on track. You should feel deeply that you can do something to improve your child's learning.

A female parent is called a MOM. Regarding education, the letters of this word could stand for "madly on a mission." A male parent is called a DAD. These letters could spell "desperate and determined." Both characterizations capture the intensity and dedication demanded of parents if they are to help their children succeed in school. All moms and dads need the passion, desire, and drive to succeed in the role of teacher in the home.

Parents can truly make a difference in their children's work in the classroom. Parents must believe this deep-down. Review the five assertions below. Recite them to yourself several times. Most of all, believe in them!

1. I am important in my child's education.

2. I can learn skills to improve my child's study habits.

3. My child needs my attention and time.

4. I am going to make a difference in my child's learning.

5. I am going to make the effort to make a difference.

Reasons for Making an Effort

In most cases, it is up to you whether your child becomes a slow, average, or above-average student. You may ask: "Why should I make the effort to make a difference?" There are many reasons. Six are given below. Pause after each and reflect on its message.

1. Because you love your child.

2. Because you care about what your child will become.

3. Because you want your child to become successful and happy.

4. Because you want your child to say fondly, "That's my mom; that's my dad."

5. Because you want to be somebody special in your child's life.

6. Because you want your child to feel good about him- or herself by succeeding in school.

Perhaps, you can think of other reasons for making an effort to work with your child on study skills. Share them with each other. To acquire insight into your relationship with your child and his or her school, complete the following exercises. You can do this alone or with others.

Give Your Child a Hand

Place your left hand on the figure on the next page as you read the following paragraphs.

Study skills can be likened to the human hand. The palm is comparable to a supportive home environment and positive parent attitudes. It serves as an anchor for all the fingers. In like manner, parents and the home serve as principal authors of a child's learning.

For the hand to function effectively, all fingers must be in working order. For students to function effectively in school, they must be skilled in certain study habits. The thumb is the most important finger on the hand. As the thumb is to the hand, reading is to school success. All learning rests on it.

The study skills represented by the other four fingers are essential for students to do well in school. Parents have a heavy responsibility to ensure that all the fingers on the "learning" hand work.

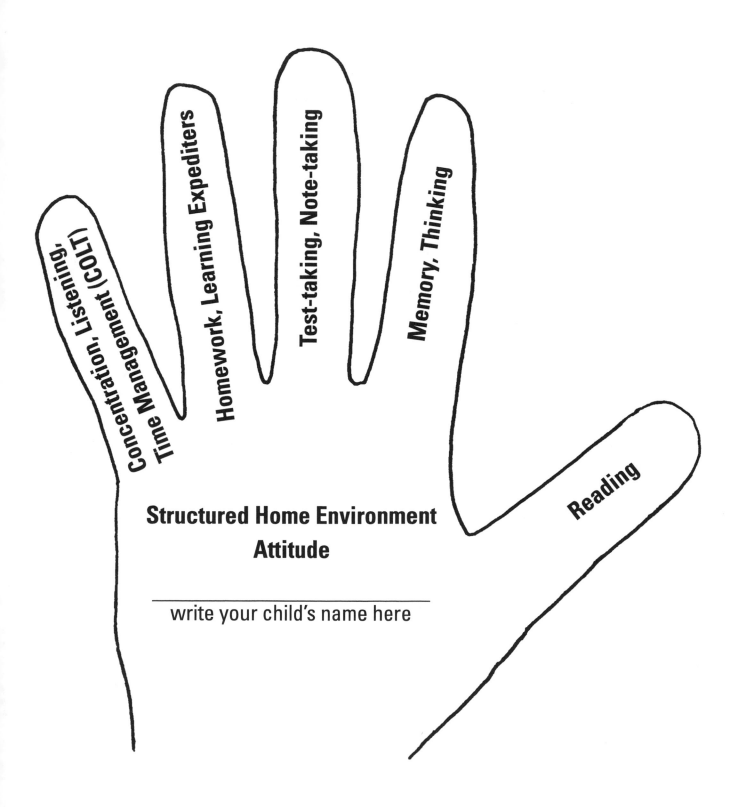

Concentration, Listening, (COLT)
Time Management

Homework, Learning Expediters

Test-taking, Note-taking

Memory, Thinking

Reading

Structured Home Environment

Attitude

write your child's name here

Parent Introspection

There is value in comparing the expectations of parents, children, and the school. Healthy relationships grow from a better understanding of each other. Parents, especially, can benefit from analyzing their wants and needs. That done, they can then design ways to meet the needs of their children.

Examine the points below. Fill in the blanks and discuss your thoughts with your children.

FIVE things your children want from you

1. _____

2. _____

3. _____

4. _____

5. _____

FOUR things you expect from your children

1. _____

2. _____

3. _____

4. _____

THREE things your children expect from school

1. _____

2. _____

3. _____

TWO things you expect from school

1. _____

2. _____

ONE thing the school expects from you

1. _____

Attitude: A Synopsis

Attitude is crucial to helping your children in school. It is the source of success and happiness in everyone's life. Attitudes arise from mental pictures people create about themselves and others. These pictures drive our behavior; they can be negative or positive. Everyone has the power to create positive pictures.

Four common questions about attitudes are given below. Review and discuss them with your children. Always be mindful that children copy their parent's attitude about everything, particularly learning.

1. What is attitude?
    A state of mind, the way you see things and feel about things. It is one of the few things in life that you can control.

2. Why is it important?
    It influences how you act and feel. It influences how you look, your degree of happiness. It influences what you will become in life and how much you will enjoy life and your children.

3. How can you develop a positive attitude?

    ❖ By being enthusiastic about life.

    ❖ By helping others.

    ❖ By respecting and being considerate of others.

    ❖ By taking pride in your work and your children.

    ❖ By learning and growing.

    ❖ By being kind.

    ❖ By always trying to do your best.

4. What develops a negative attitude?

    ❖ Always criticizing and complaining.

    ❖ Looking at the bad side of everything.

    ❖ Doing nothing.

    ❖ Refusing to help others.

    ❖ Not taking pride in your work or your children.

    ❖ Being rude.

    ❖ Not always trying to do your best.

Molding Children

Parents are at the center of a child's universe. They have a chance to mold their children. Motivational specialist Ray Maloney lists some ways to raise great children. Reflect on them. Give special attention to the last one.

- ❖ Love them.

- ❖ Listen to them.

- ❖ Challenge them.

- ❖ Limit them.

- ❖ Expect respect.

- ❖ Let them go.

- ❖ Build their self-esteem.

- ❖ Help them be community-minded.

- ❖ Develop a love of learning.

More than love is necessary to develop great students. Knowledge of learning is also necessary. But how can you show your child that you have this knowledge? One way is by developing skills to help your child improve study habits in school. Your child will look up to you and respect you for possessing such skills.

Parents as Motivators

Praising your children can motivate them to do well in school. Remember that your children's efforts as well as their performance in school deserve reinforcement. You can encourage them to work harder in the classroom with a sincere, verbal pat on the back.

It is best to vary your choice of words when complimenting your children. Using the same expression soon loses its impact. Also, it is best to praise on a regular basis and when it is truly deserved.

Many parents encourage learning in school by displaying their children's schoolwork on the refrigerator, mirror, wall, or home bulletin board. Chatting with others about how well your children are doing in school and allowing them to hear this conversation will do wonders for the way they view themselves as learners.

At the top of page 27 are expressions that you can use with your children. They can spur them to work harder in school. To this list, add others you have found effective. Share them with your neighbors and friends.

That's fantastic work; keep it up!

What a neat job!

Congratulations! You got most of it!

Wow, I'm impressed!

What you did pleases us!

I appreciate that effort!

Great, you gave it your best shot!

Way to go!

That is outstanding!

We're all proud of that!

You showed great progress!

I like the way you handled that!

Splendid, you got it!

Everyone will be proud of you!

Your work is marvelous!

A sensational try!

Superb, sharp, and awesome!

Excellent!

What encouraging statements do you find to be most effective with your child? Write them here.

A Letter of Love

You can also encourage your children in writing. The following is a brief reminder to your child of your love for him or her. It will also show your child how important his or her schoolwork is to you. Place this note on his or her bed or dresser several times a year.

> Dear _____,
>
> This is just a little note telling you that I love you. I want you to know that I expect you to do well in school. Learn as much as you can. If you need any help with your school problems, please talk to me about them. We are a team and can work together. To me, you are a very special person. Our family is so proud of you.
>
> Mom/Dad

Give Your Children an Edge

Some feel that the greatest change in education over the last half century has been the growth in parent participation in their children's school life. Teachers have tried to work more closely with parents on homework assignments; administrators have opened their doors wider to parent involvement in school affairs. More books and magazines are providing ideas for parents on how they can improve their children's learning.

There is a slogan posted in one school that says:

When Parents Participate, Students Succeed.
Strong Families Give Kids an Edge in School.

Identify three ways you are giving your children an edge in school.

1._____

2._____

3._____

Identify three additional ways you can further enhance their learning in school.

1._____

2._____

3._____

STUDY MORE, STUDY BETTER

Most children fail to do well in school because they do not study enough. Why don't they? The principal reasons are given below. Some of these reasons are from page 5 of Gary Bergreen's book, *Coping with Study Strategies.* Although published in 1990, the points are still relevant today.

Parents can do something about these problems. Examine the items below. Then answer the question under each item. Parents should discuss their responses among themselves.

1. Children fail to realize the importance of studying and schoolwork. What can parents do?

2. Children have a defeatist attitude. What can parents do?

3. Children believe education is not important. What can parents do?

4. Children are too tired, too fatigued, to do schoolwork. What can parents do?

5. Children do not have time for study because of friends, TV, and outside activities. What can parents do?

6. Children do not know how to study. What can parents do?

A WEEKLY 20-POINT PARENT CHECKUP

It is important that you show your child that you value education. Regardless of what kind of student you were, you can play a strong role in your child's school performance. A weekly checkup can remind you of your responsibilities.

There are many things you can do to help your children succeed in school. The little things you do every day will stress the importance of learning and set an example for children. To borrow from Helen Keller: "You can do almost anything you want to if you stick to it long enough."

Conduct this checkup on yourself. Post this list where you can see it constantly. Each week, identify one area that needs improvement. Reread Helen Keller's statement above.

YES   NO

____   ____   1. I talk to my child regularly about school.

____   ____   2. I keep an ample supply of reading material (books, magazines, newspapers) in my home.

____   ____   3. I often watch news programs and special event programs with my child.

____   ____   4. I frequently help my child with homework.

____   ____   5. I occasionally ask my child to look up the definition of new words or information in an encyclopedia.

____   ____   6. I set aside a special study area for my child.

____   ____   7. I often take my child to the library.

____   ____   8. I frequently read in front of my child.

____   ____   9. I make a habit of showing my child interesting articles or pictures from magazines and newspapers.

____   ____   10. I regularly attend school activities with my child.

____   ____   11. I discuss with my child messages sent home by the school.

____   ____   12. I schedule a period in the evening as homework time for my child.

____   ____   13. I see to it that noise levels are kept down during my child's homework time.

____   ____   14. I make sure my child has no health problems, such as hearing or vision difficulties, that can affect his or her learning in school.

____   ____   15. I try to ensure my child receives a balanced diet.

____   ____   16. I see that my child gets adequate rest to perform at his or her full potential in school.

____   ____   17. On a regular basis, I praise my child for both effort and achievement.

____   ____   18. I have secured a library card for my child and encourage him or her to use it.

____   ____   19. I allow my child to select books from a library or store that he or she wants me to read to him or her.

____   ____   20. I try to play educational games with my child.

PARENT CONTRACT

Working to instill a strong study ethic in our children is serious business. Promising to do this is fine, but pledging in contract form to do specific things is better.

You should talk to your friends and neighbors about making a strong commitment to become a learning facilitator. Encourage them to write their intentions in a contract. Contracts demonstrate sincerity on the part of parents to try to make a difference in their children's learning. You can discuss the contract below. Decide to whom you want to give this contract. Initial each item on the left line and sign below.

Parent Contract

_____ I will show affection toward my child every day.

_____ I will talk to my child in a patient, understanding, and caring manner.

_____ I will limit my child's television viewing time and allow him or her to watch only respectable programs.

_____ I will keep informed about what is going on in my child's school and what he or she is learning.

_____ I will ensure that my child receives sufficient sleep and goes to bed on time.

_____ I will make sure that my child is properly dressed and fed before going to school each day.

_____ I will provide a suitable time and place for my child to study every day.

_____ I will always check my child's homework assignments to see that they are completed.

Signature _____

Date _____

Parent Attitude Enhancement Activity 1

Repeat the following statement quietly to yourself 10 times:

I am important in the life of my child.

Parent Attitude Enhancement Activity 2

Shade in the letters below with a pen, pencil, or crayon. Then close your eyes and reflect on what these words really mean.

Parent Attitude Enhancement Activity 3

YOUR CHILD'S LEARNING DEPENDS ON *YOU!*

Please complete the puzzle below. The first letters in the answers are given. Use these answers to spark discussion of the parents' role in helping children learn in school. Discuss the following questions with your neighbors or friends:

❖ How do children benefit when parents lend a hand in their schoolwork?

❖ What do other people think of parents who make the effort to help their children do their very best in school?

ACROSS CLUES

3. Our most precious possession
6. A child's first teachers
7. Helps develop values and morals
8. The basic social unit in our country
9. What every child needs

DOWN CLUES

1. Necessary for a good life
2. Number of commandments
4. Most important skill in school
5. Shapes behavior

ANSWERS

ACROSS
3. Children
6. Parents
7. Religion
8. Family
9. Love

DOWN
1. Education
2. Ten
4. Reading
5. Discipline

The Home Environment

PARENT STUDY GUIDE 2

FOCUS
Converting part of the home into a study environment

PURPOSE
Learning what needs to be done to transform a place in the home into a study area for your child

SKILL
Designing a Special Study Area for your child

REFLECTION
Sharing your thoughts, before and after this lesson, on a Special Study Area for your child in the home

Before:

After:

SUPPLYING A SUPPORTIVE HOME LEARNING ENVIRONMENT

A stable home environment is fundamental to improved student learning. Parents must provide a home for children that supports learning both emotionally and physically. Homes structured so children can study will markedly increase their chance for success in school.

When children are growing up, they spend a large part of their lives in the home. They soon view their home as a living place where the family spends a lot of time together.

Seldom do children see their homes as learning places. Instead, they think of studying and learning as activities that occur in school, in the library, or in church. Home is a place where you eat, sleep, play, watch TV, and have fun. Children catch a glimpse of their home as a study place when they are required to do homework there. But when homework is taken home infrequently, children are less inclined to consider the home to be a place for study.

Parents need to cultivate respect among their children for the intellectual potential of the home. The home is a child's first and most important environment, a place where attitudes and study habits are learned. Regardless of how poor the home, it can become an educational castle if parents make an effort to design it for learning.

BECOME A LEARNING ARCHITECT

All parents can become learning architects. All they have to do is rearrange certain parts of the home. Families decorate and rearrange their homes for holidays or parties. The same can be done in the home to promote learning, the most important thing parents can do for their children. The following six steps provide suggestions for doing this.

Step 1: Set aside an area, room, or space as your child's Special Study Area (SSA). This study area can be permanent or temporary.

- ❖ **Permanent arrangement.** If there is available space that can be converted into a study area, designate it as the permanent study spot for your child. A bedroom or den is an ideal site. Let everyone in the house know that this area is an SSA and is off-limits for any activity other than study during the home's study time.

❖ **Temporary arrangement.** In crowded households, it often is difficult for parents to find a quiet study spot for their school-age children. If this is your situation, or if your house is small and no area can be used on a permanent basis for a study site, improvise the best you can. Rearrange furniture to form an isolated area to be used for your child's study area. Furniture can be returned to its original position when your child is finished studying.

Another option is to shape a large piece of cardboard or plywood into a portable partition. The idea is to use material that can be erected and taken down easily. This partition can seal off part of a bedroom or living room during your child's study time. Wherever possible, use furniture boxes that can be folded and placed around furniture to provide some privacy. These boxes can be colored and decorated by your child.

Step 2: Play up your child's Special Study Area (SSA).

❖ When your child's study site is identified, you need to stress its importance. Play it up; make it attractive. Highlight what is going on there. Make posters or signs to post on the wall, partitions, or furniture in your child's SSA. Encourage your child to decorate the signs or the site and come up with a catchy name. Some examples are:

Jeff's Study Corral	Tyrone's Brain Center
Qianna's Learning Glen	Kim's Intelligence Room
Stacey's Head Place	Joey's Study Chalet
Linda's Quiet Area	Maria's Study Retreat
Hector's Pursuit of Excellence Hut	Johnny's Machine Shop
Ben's Work Cottage	Keisha's Study Zone: Quiet!

or

"Celebrity at Work"	"Genius Working"
"Mind Is Busy"	"The Happening Place"
"Star Power Room"	"The Learning Farm"

Step 3: Check for and neutralize the enemies of learning in the home.

❖ Every home has conditions that make it difficult for a child to study. If the home is to be converted into a learning environment, parents must check for five conditions that influence learning. These are summarized by the acronym VENTTEL:

VE	Ventilation
N	Noise
T	Traffic
TE	Temperature
L	Lighting

❖ Good ventilation, temperature, and lighting are essential to good health. If a child's study area has poor air circulation, or if it is too cold or warm, parents cannot expect a child to concentrate on schoolwork. Further, poor room lighting places a strain on a child's eyes and can cause headaches and distractions.

❖ Perhaps the deadliest enemy of learning in the home is noise. Children need a quiet environment in which to do mental work. Some common noise-makers found in the home are listed below. Try to eliminate them. If you can't, at least try to reduce their noise level when children study.

Television	Dogs barking
Radios	Telephone
CDs, tapes	Playing children, inside or outside
Dishwasher/dryer/washing machine	

❖ There is another side of noise. Soothing, classical music can enhance the mood for studying. This has been a topic for many ongoing studies. To find out which melodies have a beneficial effect on learning, parents are advised to expose their children to a variety of music when they are doing their schoolwork. The parents can then determine the kinds of music that serve as a learning aid for their children.

❖ If television is used to entertain younger children, at least turn down the volume. (See "Frank Talk About Television" on page 42 for more on this subject.) If you have to talk on the phone, lower your voice. And if the other children have to play, move them farthest away from the child who is studying and always remind them to keep the noise level down. Daily posting of a "Quiet" sign outside your child's SSA might also help.

❖ Another foe of a child's learning in the home is traffic. As a parent, you should know the main traffic lanes in your home. Locate your child's SSA away from these often-used paths. The family room, TV area, kitchen table, and refrigerator are normally the most heavily traveled areas. If possible, a child's study area should never be stationed near these home traffic magnets.

Step 4: Equip your child's SSA with study supplies and equipment.

❖ Try to supply your child with a self-contained, well-equipped study environment. Make it unnecessary for your child to leave his or her SSA to hunt for items needed to study. Use the following checklist of items. If these items, or most of them, are handy, your child will not be able to find an excuse to interrupt study time.

___Paper	___Scissors	___Ruler	___Paper clips
___Pencils	___Scotch tape	___Stapler	___Pencil sharpener
___Calendar	___Dictionary	___Encyclopedias	___Eraser
___Lamp	___Desk	___Chair	___Bookcase

❖ Your child does not need a soft chair, phone, or television in order to study effectively, so do not provide these items. Do provide your child with a homework box or tray. Place it on the desk. Also, put a mailbox with your child's name on it on the desk. Put notes from you in it as well as mail that he or she might receive. This adds a business-like touch to the study area.

Step 5: With help from your child, label the drawers, shelves, and cabinets in the SSA.

❖ Some homes may not have file cabinets or bookcases to label. In that case, parents can use boxes, crates, or makeshift furniture to use as storage for study supplies.

❖ Parents can be on the lookout for discarded bookcases, old lumber, and second-hand furniture at garage sales and in shopper want ads. They are often inexpensive. Recruit your child to help you label a math cabinet, test drawers, personal library bookcase, or science shelf.

Step 6: Provide your child with a system for organizing schoolwork brought home.

❖ Some homes are in a position to provide a child with a file cabinet for organizing homework. Other homes cannot afford one. In this case, parents can convert old boxes into file shelves for organizing schoolwork. On a smaller scale, parents can acquire color-coded folders in which a child can store schoolwork for each subject. For example:

Red: Language Arts (reading, spelling, etc.)

Blue: Math

Brown: Science

Green: Social Studies

Or parents can use a letter-code system, filing homework or schoolwork under

LA for Language Arts   Sci. for Science

MA for Math   Soc. St. for Social Studies

This simple approach at home will teach a child organizational skills regarding schoolwork. These skills can be applied to the classroom as well.

The chief purpose in restructuring the home for learning is to create a climate for motivating children to study. Motivation to do well in school is linked to how well parents engineer the home to teach proper study habits to their children.

Parent Exercise 1

❖ Draw a rough map of your home. Identify major appliances and furniture. Then place an **X** by those items that interfere with your child's learning. Explore how you might handle these distractions.

Parent Exercise 2

❖ Redesign your home to make it more compatible for your child's learning. On this blueprint, show how you could move furniture or use handmade items for your child's study area. Make sure the design fits your home so that you can implement it easily.

KNOW YOUR CHILD'S LEARNING AND STUDY HABITS

One step toward improved study skills is the child's analysis of his or her learning or study habits. Your child can then focus on specific strengths and weaknesses.

Parents should sit down with their child and help him or her complete the following tables. After completing this exercise, parents should encourage the child to explain any differences between the two tables for each study habit. If expectations are higher than actual performance, these discrepancies should be addressed.

Area	In My Class, I Rank in the . . .					I Would Like to Rank in the . . .				
	Upper 10%	Upper 50%	Lower 50%	Lower 10%	Don't Know	Upper 10%	Upper 50%	Lower 50%	Lower 10%	Don't Know
Study Habits										
Reading Speed										
Reading Comprehension										
Writing										
Spelling										
Grammar										
Vocabulary										
Math										
Science										
Social Studies										
Gym/Physical Education										
Completing Homework										
Managing Class Study Time										
Listening										

FRANK TALK ABOUT TELEVISION

Television has become a symbol of American culture. There are few institutions in our country that have been studied more than television in terms of its impact on children. All media, in fact, have come to fill an enormous space in the lives of many children. A study by the Kaiser Family Foundation completed in 1999 found that 3,000 children age 2 through 18 use the media close to six hours a day. The media examined were television, computers (including computer games), recorded music, reading material, and radio. This list also shows how the types of media rank in usage by children; television is the most popular, while radio is the least popular.

According to the Kaiser Family Foundation study, there are on average three television sets in every home. A television is found in the bedrooms of one third of children under 8 years old and two thirds of youngsters over 8 years old. Two important lessons come from this study. First, the older children get, the more they use the media. Some children between 8 and 18 years old spent more than 10 hours a day on all forms of media. Second, television viewing placed well ahead of the rest of the media as a child's favorite medium. As popular and widespread as computers are, they were still not as popular as television. Reading was next to last as a child's favorite media. If you want reading to be your child's favorite pastime, start early to champion this activity over television. On the basis of these findings, it would be smart for parents to take the following steps:

1. Remove all television sets from children's bedrooms.

2. Set up reasonable rules for watching television.

Television is a great information and entertainment medium. However, its potential to interfere with learning is enormous. It can be a friend to learning if used wisely, or it can be learning's most formidable adversary. On the positive side, television can draw the family together, provide leisure-time entertainment, and teach through its use of color, graphics, and motion. Every year, television programming includes a variety of fascinating educational programs. Parents should make it a point to watch these programs with their children and to discuss their contents.

On the negative side, television can expose children to a heavy diet of raw violence and mindless commercials—hardly subjects that develop the intellectual power of children. A 1992 study by the American Psychological Association reported that before children complete elementary school, they will have watched 8,000 murders and 100,000 additional incidents of television violence. By the time these children are 18 years old, the figures jump to 40,000 murders and 200,000 acts of violence.

Most appalling is the "separation time" that plagues American families. Not enough time is spent together. In newspaper reports in 1999, David Walsh from the National Institute on Media and the Family estimated that the time children spend watching television and video games is eleven times the amount of time they spend with their parents. He says that the violence, sex, and other vices on television, movie screens, and computers seen daily by children have a retarding effect on their growing brain. Parents must keep the following in mind:

> ## BE ZEALOUS GATEKEEPERS OF
> ## WHAT YOUR CHILDREN WATCH
> ## AND HOW THEY SPEND THEIR TIME.

Bad television has been recognized widely as a serious problem for children. In 1990, Congress enacted the Children's Television Law. It limits television advertising to 12 minutes for every hour of children's programs during the week and 1½ minutes less on weekends. It also mandates that television shows for children contain some educational value. If they do not, the networks face losing their license. Many critics doubt whether this legislation has upgraded television shows for children.

Television viewing can result in lazy bodies and even lazier minds. It keeps children from reading, conversing, and reflecting. It also has been found to interfere with sleep, good eating habits, hobbies, and schoolwork. What is more, much of what is programmed on television can lead to antisocial behavior among young children. No wonder many educators are sounding the alarm that television is corrupting children.

A real danger of television is the false expectations it can create. Television is primarily an entertainment industry. Schools are an education business. Television can spoil children by deluding them into thinking that schools should entertain them in the same way. Compared to TV, children find schools boring. Understandably, teachers find it tough to compete with the action-packed, artificial world of television. Besides, TV viewing is a passive activity; viewers do not have to lift a finger, unlike what is required in school.

The popular television watchdog, the National Institute on Media and the Family, lists on its website a number of studies accusing television of wasting the time of children and extolling violence (see www.mediafamily.org). These studies reveal that the average child 2–11 years of age views television at least 28 hours every week. By mid-adolescence, the child will have watched a total of 15,000 hours of television.

Given these figures, it is not surprising that television is raising many children. Some children pay more attention to television than to their parents. They spend more time watching TV than talking to family members. These children receive their main education from television. Many form their values, attitudes, and behavior from what they see on TV. In the final analysis, this medium becomes surrogate parents to children and their substitute teacher.

Most households do not have rules governing TV viewing by children. All parents need to lay down such rules. Two are particularly critical. One should identify which TV shows are strictly forbidden. Those shows with gratuitous sex and violence could be put on this list.

The second rule on children's TV viewing should answer the questions of "when" and "how much." It is reasonable for parents to limit a child's television time during the school week. Parents should see to it that the child does the following things:

1. Spends more time doing schoolwork than watching TV during the week.

2. Completes homework and school assignments before extended TV viewing.

Television viewing takes time away from schoolwork. Do you know how much time your child spends spellbound by the "Idiot Box"?

Track your child's TV viewing time for one week using the TV viewing log on the next page.

TV VIEWING LOG

Child's Name _____

Week of _____

SHOWS WATCHED	TIME SPENT WATCHING SHOWS				
	1 hour	2 hours	3 hours	4 hours	5+ hours
Monday					
Tuesday					
Wednesday					
Thursday					
Friday					
Saturday					
Sunday					

Total Time Watching TV _____

TV shows can be dominated by

❖ comedy

❖ crime

❖ family life sitcoms

❖ investigation

❖ music

❖ news and information

❖ sex

❖ talk and conversation

❖ violence

Analysis of the Kind of Shows Your Child Watched

_____

_____

_____

_____

_____

_____

_____

_____

Study Skills (COLT)

PARENT STUDY GUIDE 3

FOCUS   COLT: Concentration, Listening, and Time-management skills—building blocks to effective learning

PURPOSE   Acquiring knowledge about COLT and its impact on learning

SKILL   Planning ways to help your child concentrate, listen, and manage time in class

REFLECTION   Sharing your thoughts, before and after this lesson, on the ideas examined relating to COLT

Before:

After:

WHAT PARENTS NEED TO KNOW ABOUT CONCENTRATION, LISTENING, AND TIME MANAGEMENT

WHAT IS CONCENTRATION?

Concentration is a shortcut to learning. It is a skill anyone can learn and a skill that can be sharpened through practice.

To concentrate means to pay close attention, to engage in deep thought, to become engrossed in something, to maintain interest over a period of time. Some children have strong powers of concentration. Others do not; they find it difficult to stay focused on a subject very long.

WHAT CAUSES CONCENTRATION PROBLEMS?

Many parents become alarmed over the inability of their children to pay attention. So do teachers. They frequently note that the minds of students wander easily into daydreaming. Everywhere, the problem of student inattention impedes learning. The causes of this problem can be either physical or environmental.

Physical Causes

Children with severe attention-span problems may have a physical disorder. This disorder is due to a specific brain abnormality called attention deficit hyperactivity disorder (ADHD). For short, it is often referred to as hyperactivity. It affects 3% to 5% of all children.

The smallest distraction, such as a singing bird or passing car, interrupts the concentration of a child with ADHD. It could be the reason why the child misbehaves in school or earns failing grades. Medication, behavior modification, and therapy are used in treating this problem. Parent/teacher support groups for ADHD children have cropped up around the country Interested parents can contact the group in their immediate area if they need information or advice on this problem.

Children afflicted with ADHD struggle with schoolwork. They tend to fidget, be overly energetic, get into things, and have trouble concentrating. To concentrate on their studies, children with ADHD need a quiet place to study with few distractions, no friends around them, and close supervision by parents or teachers.

Parents should not blame themselves for their child's concentration problems if they are due to ADHD. This problem is not the result of poor parenting. If parents suspect a physical basis to their child's attention difficulties in the home or school, they should check with their physician.

Environmental Causes

The concentration problems of most children can be traced to environment and habit. The world of children is filled with distractions. Almost everywhere, children are bombarded by stimulants of all sorts: TV, music, friends, parties, traffic—the list goes on. Concentration is the ability to shut out distractions. Many children have not learned to do this.

WHAT CAN PARENTS DO TO REMOVE DISTRACTIONS?

Teaching children to block out distractions and focus their mind on what needs to be learned takes time and patience. Building a child's ability to concentrate comes in phases. The formula below provides a strategy for parents to increase their child's concentration powers. Work through the phases slowly, one at a time.

Phase 1: Identify specific distractions in the home.

❖ For example, under "noise," you can identify barking dogs, television, radio, dishwasher, dryer, washing machine, or telephone.

anxiety	hunger	stresses
company	light	temperature
fatigue	noise	_____
fighting	siblings	_____
friends	snacks/food	_____

Circle those distractions that you can do something about. Place an **X** next to those distractions that you cannot change.

Phase 2: Identify distractions in your child's classes.

❖ Get this information from your child, his or her classmates and friends, or other parents whose children are in your child's class.

Distraction 1. _____

Distraction 2. _____

Distraction 3. _____

Distraction 4. _____

Distraction 5. _____

Now that you know what can interfere with your child's learning, think about what you can do to eliminate these distractions. Now move to phase three.

Phase 3: Describe ways to eliminate a child's study distractions at home and in school.

For distractions at home, I can:

1. _____

2. _____

3. _____

4. _____

For distractions at school, I can:

1. _____

2. _____

3. _____

4. _____

The last phase in a parent's effort to develop a child's concentration skills takes the most time. This involves using specific strategies while working closely with a child. Below is a list of parent strategies aimed at raising a child's level of concentration. Some of these ideas are taken from page 9 of Gary Bergreen's book, *Coping with Study Strategies,* 1990. He refers to them as "Study Warm-Ups."

Phase 4: Use parent-led exercises to improve a child's concentration skills.

❖ To gain cooperation, especially with young children, make a game of concentration. Play these games with your child often.

Game 1: Sit in a chair. Scan the room to see its details. Ask the question, "What is in this room?" Then close your eyes. Mentally recall or name the objects in the room. When finished, open your eyes and write down the names of the objects that you recall. Next, look around the room and see what you remembered and what you forgot. Repeat this game to see if you can remember more.

Game 2: In 30 seconds, recite as many colors, states, songs, furry animals, pop singers, football players, or other things as you can.

Game 3: In a picture or book of pictures, count all objects that begin with the letters "th" and end in the letters "ion."

Game 4: When examining a comic book (or newspaper), identify the good things that happen to people; then identify the bad things.

Game 5: Give a prize, present, hug, or special privilege to your children if they can describe what they smell when you are cooking (or taste when they are eating different foods), what they see on the way to school, or what they hear on the street corner.

Game 6: Make a contest of having your child provide as much information as possible about the following. Invite him or her to explain each in detail.

- an experience

- a friend

- a toy or game

- what was learned in school

- a picture, poster, or sign recently seen

Game 7: Have your child practice doing two things at one time. It is tough to concentrate when required to do several things at one time. Practicing to perform several things at one time can strengthen one's power of concentration. Try these exercises with a friend or neighbor. Then try them with your child.

- On a sheet of paper, write the alphabet backwards; or the months of the year in reverse order; or the numbers 50 to 1, backwards; or the main holidays in America, starting with the month of December and backtracking to January.

- In teams of two, parents should talk to each other at the same time about what each did yesterday. The simultaneous, two-way conversation should last 60 seconds. Set an alarm clock to notify both parties when the time is up. Each parent should then tell what they heard the other say.

❖ The American Automobile Association (AAA) has published several learning materials that can increase a child's observation and concentration skills while on trips in a car with you. They are *Truck Games*, *Road Signs Game*, and *Travel Activity Book*. These publications contain activities that teach travel, map, language, and geography skills. They can be picked up for a minimal cost at many local AAA offices.

REVIEW OF CONCENTRATION

Children can improve their concentration powers in the same way that they can become more accomplished musicians or basketball players: practice. Parents have a responsibility to see to it that their children practice concentration. They can make it easier for a child to concentrate by heeding the following reminders.

Concentration Reminders

1. Have your child study in the same place every day (so that studying becomes routine).

2. Have your child study in a quiet place (solitude increases concentration).

3. Convert a room into a "study center" (equip it with learning or school supplies).

4. Remember that

    ❖ a study area should have suitable ventilation, light, and temperature.

    ❖ a study area should be free of clutter, noise, and distractions.

5. Remind your child to prop up reading or study materials. When on an angle, they are easier to read and understand.

6. Urge your child to study only one task at a time. Remind him or her to finish it before taking on another task. Permit a snack or a call to a friend only after the first task is done.

7. Encourage your child to get a drink, snack, and rest before studying. It is hard to concentrate when thirsty, hungry, or tired!

8. Make it a habit to ask your child the reasons for studying a lesson. Insist that he or she explain its purpose (for example, to find out about the causes of the Civil War in a social studies class or to learn how to add two-digit numbers in a math class).

LISTENING SKILLS

Listening is a close companion to concentration. It is so vital to learning that some states and schools require teachers to test students on their listening skills. One needs to concentrate to listen well. Much of what is learned in school comes through listening. Many children do poorly in school because they are poor listeners.

It is important for all parents to make sure that their child receives a hearing test before starting school to determine if he or she has a hearing impairment. Your child's hearing should then be checked occasionally as he or she progresses through school. Hearing well is important to listening and academic success.

Hearing is not the same as listening. Just because one hears words does not mean the message is understood. Listening takes practice and concentration; hearing does not. Listening takes effort; hearing does not. And listening requires the active participation of the listener; hearing does not.

Children often are accused of not listening in class. When this happens, their schoolwork suffers. If parents do their part at home in polishing their child's listening skills, they will make it easier for the child to listen in school.

FIVE PARENT RULES ON LISTENING

There are five rules that can guide parents in their efforts to improve their children's listening skills. Study them carefully before applying them at home.

Rule 1: Talk about the importance of listening in school.

a. How listening helps a child:

 ❖ The child will understand what is going on.

 ❖ The child will learn the material in class and earn good grades.

 ❖ The child will avoid mistakes in schoolwork.

 ❖ The child will make friends and be well-liked, since everyone likes a careful listener.

b. How not listening hurts a child:

 ❖ The child will fail to understand what is going on.

 ❖ The child will fail to learn the material in class and will not earn good grades.

 ❖ The child could make serious mistakes and be hurt. (If a child fails to listen and take medicine when sick, he or she could become sicker.)

c. Why we listen:

Listening is one of the four communication skills. The others are reading, writing, and talking. Of these four, listening is the most neglected. Most children learn to listen on their own. Because it is rarely taught in school, parents need to prepare their children for school by teaching their children how to listen at home.

Explain to your children what listening is. To listen means to pay attention, to note carefully. Explain that it comes primarily through one of our five senses: hearing. Explain, too, that other senses are involved in the listening process. For example, the expression we see on the face of the person talking will help us listen to what he or she is saying. Next, analyze with your children why people listen.

1. For enjoyment, pleasure, and entertainment:

 ❖ *music, TV, radio, conversations*

2. For information:

 ❖ *instructions, directions*

 ❖ *to find out about the world, life, important events (newscasts, lectures, speakers, etc.)*

3. For learning and understanding:

     ❖ *listening to friends, parents, leaders, etc.*

     ❖ *listening to teachers*

     ❖ *making sense out of information*

     ❖ *analyzing problems*

     ❖ *putting together ideas*

Explain that listening to teachers in the classroom can help students learn

     a. big ideas

     b. details

     c. skills

     d. procedures and processes

Explain that listening leads to learning when a student

     a. *understands* important points

     b. *reviews* important points

     c. *reflects on* these important points

Rule 2: Establish what kind of listener your child has been in class.

     a. Ask your child.

     b. Ask the child's teacher.

     c. Ask the child's playmates, classmates.

     d. Ask yourself: "What kind of listener is my child at home?"

Rule 3: Administer a listening test to your child.

Review the 10-Point Listening Habits Checklist on page 55. As you tabulate the results, see if they tell you anything about your child's listening habits. Examine each individual response with your child and consider how it helps or hurts him or her as student. If your child decides that a response will affect his or her work as a student, ask the child what might be done to change the situation.

10-POINT LISTENING HABITS CHECKLIST

You and your child should complete this checklist together. Some of the ideas were borrowed from page 5 of the book *Communications Skills: The Art of Listening,* Teacher's Guide, published by the Educational Dimensions Group in 1984.

1. Are you easily distracted by someone else when the teacher talks to you?

   ❑ YES   ❑ NO

2. Do you fake attention to get by or just to be polite?

   ❑ YES   ❑ NO

3. Does your mind often wander when the teacher talks to you?

   ❑ YES   ❑ NO

4. When others are talking, do you interrupt?

   ❑ NEVER   ❑ SELDOM   ❑ OFTEN   ❑ ALWAYS

5. Do you close your eyes while the teacher talks to the class?

   ❑ YES   ❑ NO

6. When you listen to the teacher, do you fidget, doodle, or express other nervous habits?

   ❑ YES   ❑ NO

7. When you do not understand what a teacher says, do you ask him or her to repeat it?

   ❑ NEVER   ❑ SELDOM   ❑ OFTEN   ❑ ALWAYS

8. When you listen in class, do you ever change your facial expression?

   ❑ YES   ❑ NO

9. Do you prefer to listen to main ideas or details?

   ❑ MAIN IDEAS   ❑ DETAILS

10. Do you tend to write down what you hear so you will not forget it?

   ❑ YES   ❑ NO

Rule 4: Teach your children the "listening pose" (how to position parts of their body so that they are more receptive to listening).

Instruct your child to watch a person who is listening intently to a speaker, to a TV or radio program, or to a friend in conversation. Have your child describe the position of the person's head, back, hands, eyes, and legs.

Observe a football player awaiting the snap of the ball or a violinist on the verge of playing. How do they position parts of their body to maximize their performance? Good listeners sit up straight with head bent forward, make strong eye contact, use their hands to take notes or fold them, and keep their legs close together. People slumping over, stroking their hair, and gazing around the room hardly make good listeners. Good listeners form a "listening pose" to increase their capacity to listen and learn.

Rule 5: Tell your children to ask their teacher to repeat what they do not understand.

When a child listens carefully to a teacher and does not understand the main points of a lesson, he or she should not feel embarrassed to ask a teacher to repeat what was said. That is why a teacher is in the classroom—to make sure children understand the lesson.

REVIEW OF LISTENING

Below is a review of ideas as well as additional suggestions for parents to consider in working with their children on listening skills:

1. Play music to your children when they are young, even when they are still in the crib. Soft, melodic sounds—like those in light classical music—are mentally stimulating. Some are convinced that such music has the potential to increase a child's capacity to learn listening skills.

2. Help your child understand that good listeners take turns talking; good listeners do not interrupt others.

3. Listen to your child at home; set an example in listening.

    ❖ Let your child finish a sentence; do not cut him or her off or interrupt.

    ❖ Maintain eye contact.

    ❖ Display a pleasant disposition.

    ❖ Show interest in what your child says.

    ❖ Indicate to your child that you are a good listener.

    ❖ Model a good "listening pose" for your child.

4. Give your child instructions or directions to do something, and make sure they are carried out exactly as you directed.

5. Ask your child to repeat or rephrase what was said to him or her moments ago, including both the big ideas and the details.

6. Watch TV with your children and ask them to jot down or talk about what they saw or heard.

7. Ask children, when traveling on a school bus, to listen to what they hear along the road.

8. Show children pictures from newspapers or magazines, and then ask them to describe what they saw.

9. Ask children, while watching movies, TV programs, or videotapes, to summarize for you what they heard, including both the big ideas and the details.

10. Urge children to pay attention in school because you will expect them to review what they learned, did, or studied during the day.

11. Request that children listen to teachers and repeat their favorite expressions or their jokes.

12. Tell stories to your children. Encourage them to listen closely so that they can tell you what they liked most about a story and what they liked least about a story.

13. Urge your child to listen to cues from the teacher about the important things to study and remember. These cues include

    ❖ definitions given by the teacher

    ❖ examples given by the teacher

    ❖ teacher repetition of points

    ❖ topics that the teacher spends most of his or her time on

    ❖ materials reviewed by teacher

14. Have your child listen to a radio newscast. Ask your child to recite for you what the newscaster was talking about (topic) and the "guts" (details) of the report.

15. Show a large picture to your child. Describe different parts of the picture. Put the picture down. Then ask your child to draw the same picture that you described.

Last-Ditch Efforts to Get Your Child to Listen to You

Parents frequently become frustrated when their children do not listen at home or school. In this case, dramatic steps need to be taken. The following practices have the potential to grab attention and shock a child out of poor listening habits. Their purpose is to teach a lesson about the importance of listening. Try them and see if they work for you.

1.   Write a letter to your child, mentioning what you like about him or her. At the same time, indicate how unhappy you become when he or she does not listen to you. Ask him or her to pay attention to you when you talk. That way your child will learn more and show others how grownup he or she is. End by requesting that your child write you a letter in return that responds to your letter.

OR

2.   When your child is old enough, give your child the cold treatment when he or she refuses to listen to you. Ignore the child when he or she talks to you. When he or she becomes frustrated and implores you to respond, explain that you are behaving just as your child does. Explain that you feel the same when you are not listened to.

   ❖   Ask if your child likes it when you do not listen.

   ❖   Ask if not listening to you helps him or her. Does it make life easier or more pleasant?

OR

3.   Select a large grocery bag or cardboard box, one that easily fits over your head. Cut out a square in the middle of one side of the bag or box, the size of a large TV screen. Draw pictures of knobs on the side, bottom, or top of the bag or box so that it looks like a TV set. Write "TV" on the bag or box. Fit the bag or box over your head so your face appears in the hole. When your child does not listen or when you want him or her to pay attention, talk through the TV screen. As though you were on "television," say, "May I have your attention, now?" This will startle your child and create a humorous scene that will result in a conversation about paying attention.

TIME MANAGEMENT

Time wasted is time lost forever. It is a precious commodity. There is just so much time in a person's life. Everyone has the same amount of time in a 24-hour day. Most are free to decide how to use it.

Children are not as conscious about the importance of time as adults. More often than not, they take it for granted. Children are seldom taught how to manage their time.

Time management is a term that is popular today. Many consider it the key to improved production on the job as well as in school. Time management means making the best use of one's time. For students, it means managing their study time and their work habits in order to accomplish a learning task.

Good students are skilled at managing their school and homework time. This skill suggests that these students have control over their lives. They can get their work done on their own. They do not have to depend on others.

The place to begin teaching a child to manage study time in school is in the home. Parents can follow a five-step program to ensure that a child learns this skill.

Step 1: Help your child understand the importance of time.

Your job as a parent is to increase your child's awareness of the importance of time. There are several ways in which parents can do this:

❖ Challenge your child to figure out which person has the most time in the world (we all have the same amount).

❖ Ask your child how their classmates use their time.

❖ With the help of your child, look up what an encyclopedia or other general reference says about time and how people have kept track of time.

❖ Have your child calculate how much time he or she presently spends on
(a) sleeping, (b) eating, (c) playing, (d) watching TV, and (e) doing schoolwork.

❖ Explore with your child how much time he or she should spend on the above activities and why.

❖ Ask your child to explain how he or she can avoid wasting time and get the most out of studying.

Step 2: Discuss with your child the benefits of organizing time for play and schoolwork.

Wise use of your child's study time will give him or her certain advantages. Sit down with your child and talk about these advantages. Be sure to point out that good things happen to people when they manage their time effectively, especially in school. Conversely, bad things happen to people who waste their time. What are these good things? Some of the ones listed below are taken from page 35 of Herman Ohme's book, *Learn How to Learn Study Skills,* published by California Education Plan in 1986. When children use study time wisely, they will

❖ work more productively
❖ obtain better grades
❖ remember more
❖ impress teachers
❖ feel better about themselves
❖ earn the respect of friends and classmates
❖ develop brainpower

❖ have more time to take it easy
❖ meet the deadlines to get things done
❖ be able to study more effectively
❖ find more time to play
❖ feel more motivated
❖ better please their parents
❖ be more in control of their lives

Ask your child: What bad things can happen to people who waste their time? Give examples of wasted time.

Step 3: Allow your child to do small chores around the house according to a time schedule.

Home chore schedules discipline a child for organizing schoolwork schedules later on. Children should be given the opportunity to help out in the home and to get their work done on time. With your child's help, design a chore schedule like the one below.

A CHILD'S HOME CHORE SCHEDULE

DAY	CHORE	TIME
Monday	Take out garbage	by 6:00 p.m.
Tuesday	Feed goldfish	by 7:00 a.m.
Wednesday	(free)	
Thursday	Clean bedroom	by 8:00 p.m.
Friday	Run family errand	at 7:00 p.m.
Saturday	Baby-sit	at 3:00 p.m.
Sunday	(free)	

Step 4: Give your child a variety of family experiences in planning time.

Other ways in which children can learn about the value of time and how to plan its use are noted below:

❖ Children should be included in planning experiences close to home, such as a vacation; a trip to the zoo, museum, or shopping mall; a birthday party; and communicating with friends or pen pals.

❖ Have your child keep a daily log for one week (in a notebook or on loose-leaf paper stapled together). Instruct children to keep track of how they spend time. These entries can make the child more conscious of time through the study of the pattern of time use throughout the week. Making a schedule and keeping a log enable your child to take control of the day. This also teaches time management skills. When necessary, help your child write down the time for the following activities in this "Weekly Planning Log."

WEEKLY PLANNING LOG

Child's Name _____

Week of _____

	Wake up	Breakfast	Start School a.m.	Recess	School Lunch p.m.	Homework	Supper	TV	Bedtime
Monday									
Tuesday									
Wednesday									
Thursday									
Friday									
Saturday									
Sunday									

Step 5: Teach your child to budget work time in school.

Once children learn how to account for family time, it will be easier for them to plan for study time. Work with your child to plan the amount of time to allocate to schoolwork. When finished, help your child design a schedule of study time. Learning to do this at home will transfer to your child's classroom. You can give your child a copy of the following form to help track and budget time.

TIME BUDGETED PER DAY (in minutes)

Subject or Class	Monday	Tuesday	Wednesday	Thursday	Friday
Reading					
Writing					
Science					
Social Studies					
Art					
Others					

Now, reach an agreement with your child on the sequence or order in which these subjects should be studied in school. Help your child determine

❖ whether he or she studies best in the morning or afternoon

❖ when his or her energy level is highest and when it is lowest

❖ whether he or she is more comfortable studying the toughest or easiest subject first

❖ how much of a study break is best for him or her (Some say for every hour a child studies, he or she should take a 5- to 10-minute break. The age of a child determines this.)

Check on your child to see that he or she keeps books, pencils, and other school supplies close at hand. This will eliminate the need (or excuse) for the child to interrupt study time to look for study items.

Do your part in ensuring that your children stay healthy. When children feel good, they will have the energy to deal daily with schoolwork and manage study time. Cut down on sugar and salt in a child's diet. Make sure your child gets enough sleep, exercise, and playtime. These health conditions will speed the journey toward becoming an independent learner.

REVIEW OF TIME MANAGEMENT

A student's time-management plan is only good if it can be put into action. Parents need to see that it is. You can do this by working daily with your child in organizing his or her time. The main object is to produce an independent learner who uses time wisely and completes required schoolwork. As children become skilled in managing time, parents can reduce their time supervising their children's time.

In review, you should use the following strategies:

1. Help your child understand the importance of time and how it is spent in the home.

2. Be sure your child keeps track of study time.

3. Encourage your child to evaluate his or her use of time in school.

4. Review daily at first, then periodically, how your child uses his or her study time in school.

5. Question regularly what your child has to do and the time needed to do it.

6. Be sure your child keeps an up-to-date assignment log for schoolwork, or help your child design a calendar of important learning events, pinpointing dates for tests, projects, reports, papers, and homework.

7. Remind your child to do one thing at a time, to study one subject at a time.

Homework and Learning Expediters

PARENT STUDY GUIDE 4A

FOCUS	Parents and homework
PURPOSE	Learning about the part homework plays in learning and the role of parents in homework
SKILL	Helping a child get the most out of homework
REFLECTION	Sharing your thoughts, before and after this lesson, on homework assigned to your child

Before:

After:

PARENT STUDY GUIDE 4B

FOCUS   Learning expediters: teachers, textbooks, other students, and computers

PURPOSE   Understanding how these learning expediters can be used to promote learning

SKILL   Showing a child ways to learn from teachers, textbooks, other students, and computers

REFLECTION   Sharing your thoughts, before and after this lesson, on these learning expediters

Before:

After:

HOMEWORK

ROAD TO SCHOOL SUCCESS

Homework is related to student achievement. Students who do their homework—and do it well—function more effectively in the classroom. In addition, they do better on tests. It is no secret that the more time students spend on homework, the better they do in school. Homework is definitely linked to school success.

Some studies show that American students do not spend as much time on homework as students in other countries. How much homework a child should do depends on age and physical and mental condition, as well as school policy. In 2000, the National PTA gave its view on homework time. First-graders should spend 10 minutes a day on homework. Homework time should increase 10 minutes a day per grade level. For example, sixth-graders should spend 60 minutes daily on school assignments.

Informal surveys reveal that the time American students spend on homework varies. According to the 1990 book, *Tools for Learning: A Guide to Teaching Study Skills,* by M. B. Gall and others, on average, daily homework time is about 15 minutes in primary grades, 30 minutes in upper elementary grades, 45 to 75 minutes in middle school, and 60 to 120 minutes in high school. Contrast this with Japan where three- and four-year-olds spend several hours each day to improve their chances of being admitted to kindergarten.

Numerous studies paint an alarming picture of homework in American high schools. The main reason American students take a back seat to students elsewhere, according to the National Commission on Excellence in Education, is that they are lazy with their homework. This study cited that two-thirds of American high school students do not spend even an hour on homework each day. Still other studies show that television viewing ranks far ahead of homework as the choice of high school students in their after-school time.

Parents can brighten this homework picture. In the end, a child's attitude toward homework is molded by the home. Parents can help by understanding the place that homework has in learning and what they can do in the home to support it. To begin, there are four questions parents need to answer about homework:

1. **What is homework?**

    Homework is schoolwork a child is assigned to do outside the classroom, normally at home, and which is not supervised by the teacher.

2. **What are reasons for assigning homework?** There are six major reasons:

    a.   It reinforces classroom learning.

    b.   It promotes self-discipline.

    c.   It teaches time management practices.

    d.   It cultivates positive work habits and increases retention.

    e.   It allows parents to get involved in their child's education and learn about what is being taught to their child in school.

    f.   It helps students pick up things on their own and become independent learners.

3. **What should parents know about their child's homework?**

First and foremost, parents should get information about their child's school homework policy. Many school systems have a written policy regarding homework. This policy defines homework and mandates the amount of time that students should devote to homework. What is your school's homework policy?

My school's homework policy is _____

_____

My school's homework policy requires the following specific amount of time that students should spend on homework ___daily/___weekly (check one).

_____ for grades K-3   _____ for middle school, junior high
_____ for grades 4-6   _____ for senior high school

Second, parents should know about the homework requirements of their child's teacher. What are your child's teacher's expectations about homework?

My child's teacher's homework requirements are _____

_____

_____

4. **How can parents help their children with homework?**

In many ways!

First, talk to your child about homework. Mention that learning does not stop when children leave school. Explain how homework extends the school day, giving them more time to finish their school assignments.

Second, show an interest in your child's homework assignments. Inquire about these assignments—if they are difficult, what they teach the child, when they are going to be completed. Be sure to examine the schoolwork your child brings home. Even if you do not understand it, review it.

Third, do not do the homework for your child. Homework is your child's job. Your job is to check on your child to make sure that he or she is doing his or her homework. You should also review what was done. Answer questions, clarify directions, read instructions, and help him or her understand the assignments. But let the child do the work. Try to make it a practice of helping your child with homework every night.

Fourth, convince your child to contact a friend or a teacher for help when he or she is having trouble with homework assignments.

Fifth, help your child organize homework assignments so that they can be completed on time. A homework log can teach wise use of time and how to organize homework. Homework logs can be set up for a day or a week. Zero in on those subjects with which your child is having difficulty. Homework on those subjects should receive special attention. An example of such a log is found on the following page.

Sixth, establish rules in the home for doing homework. Identify a quiet homework site and set up a homework schedule. A homework schedule helps a student ease into a groove for study. It teaches a sense of responsibility and self-discipline. A study routine can be a powerful antidote to procrastination.

Require that homework be done at the same time each day. Of course, exceptions can be made because of special activities and circumstances. But homework should be made a daily routine at home. Also, make sure that your child's homework gets done. Make it a practice of asking to see homework and congratulating your child for his or her efforts.

Seventh, share your ideas on homework with your child's teacher. Many teachers are free to set up their own homework policies. Most are willing to listen to a parent's advice on this subject.

Eighth, make a homework sign that you can set on a table or attach to a door or desk. Let your child help you make this sign. When it is displayed, it signals "work time."

HOMEWORK LOG

Day/Week of _____

Note:	Reading/Writing	Science	Social Studies	Math
What I Need to Do				
What I Need to Know				
Where to Get Information				
When Assignment Is Due				
Important Words/ Ideas to Know				

Ninth, consider these points:

❖ Most children need time to unwind after school and before doing homework; give them the opportunity for playtime.

❖ Children have trouble concentrating when they are hungry, dirty, tired, or bloated with food that is high in sugar, caffeine, and fat.

❖ Children need breaks from homework study time; a 5-minute break for each half-hour of study time is reasonable; the age of a child determines the duration of study breaks.

❖ Some experts say it is best for a student to study the most difficult assignments first, when the student is fresh, and study the least difficult last.

❖ If a child does not bring homework home at least once a week, suspect something; it is a parent's job to find out why.

Last, a parent can help a child with homework by following these "10 Homework Commandments."

  I: Thou shall know your child's school's homework policy, including the homework "hotline" that many schools have set up for students and parents. Find out if your child's school system has such a resource. If so, write the phone number here: _____.

  II: Thou shall always show interest in the homework your child brings home.

 III: Thou shall not assume responsibility for doing a child's homework. This is a child's responsibility. Your responsibility is to see that it gets done.

 IV: Thou shall designate a homework site in your home and supply it with materials needed to carry out homework assignments.

  V: Thou shall ask, at least once a week, to review the homework completed by your child so that you stay informed about the homework he or she does.

 VI: Thou shall ensure that your child makes up all work not completed because of illness or absence from school.

 VII: Thou shall not argue with a child over homework but, instead, shall impress on him or her the fact that homework is the job of a student—like work is the job of an adult.

VIII: Thou shall ask of your child how things are going during homework sessions.

 IX: Thou shall provide occasional rewards for children who do their homework responsibly.

  X: Thou shall establish the priority of homework after school, seeing to it that homework comes first—before friends, television, music, play, etc.

A PARENT PRIMER ON HOMEWORK

Not all children need parental assistance in doing their homework. Especially as they grow older, children tend to depend less on parents.

Many students have poor homework habits. Some daydream when doing homework assignments; they fail to finish what they begin; they are easily distracted from sticking to their homework; some even refuse to do their homework. Parents should expect some of these problems to arise as their children navigate through school.

Fights often occur between parent and child over homework. These can be avoided if parents design a plan to deal with homework problems in advance.

There is no silver bullet for inducing a child to do homework. However, the four guidelines below can ease the tension that comes with homework. They have been drawn from the advice of homework experts. Some of these ideas were cited earlier.

1. **Provide conditions at home that enable a child to do homework.** Make sure a homework time slot is established in the home. Establish a starting and stopping time for homework. This will help a child plan time more effectively. Homework should be done at the same time every day so it becomes a daily routine. Establish a special study site, a child's very own place, for homework. Stock this site with necessary school supplies.

2. **Highlight the importance of homework.** Give it top billing in the home. Make a poster or sign that says: "Quiet, Homework Time." Post it daily when it is your child's time for homework. This serves as a homework "bell," a signal to start studying in the home.

3. **Use homework time to do parent "homework" alongside your child.** Let your child see you engrossed in some type of mental work. Read a book, make out checks for your bills, work a crossword puzzle, write a letter, etc. This will motivate your child to get into the mood for homework activity.

4. **Frequently offer your child something nice immediately after finishing homework.** Immediate reinforcements tend to be more effective than delayed ones. Reward your child by letting him or her have a snack, watch television, make a telephone call to a friend, play a video game, or watch a movie. Later on, reduce the frequency of such rewards.

Be sure to reward effort if the homework is not completed for a legitimate reason.

HOMEWORK ENCOUNTERS

Parents frequently become frustrated in battling their children over homework. The more parents scream at children to do their homework, the more children will resist. Two rules should guide parents in homework skirmishes with their children.

First, do not yell or blow up when children argue over homework. Instead, set a good example by remaining calm. Talk in a controlled, firm manner. Reasonable communication is a parent's best ally.

Second, never use homework as punishment. And never punish a child for not doing homework. The conventional wisdom today is that the homework war is won with love, not punishment. That is a powerful idea.

COMMON HOMEWORK IRRITANTS

Below is a list of four irritants that give parents the most homework headaches with their children. Some solutions are offered for pain relief. See if they work with your children.

Irritant 1: Your child fails to do homework because he or she forgot the assignment.

Solution: Require that your child recite to you all homework assignments for the day. Check daily on your child to see that he or she remembers homework assignments, then less often as he or she shows that it gets done.

Encourage your children to suggest that their teacher write the daily assignments on the blackboard (if he or she does not already do this). This way, assignments will always be in full view of your children. More importantly, it will eliminate a common reason children give for not doing their homework assignments.

Irritant 2: Your child cannot keep track of homework assignments.

Solution: Encourage your child to keep a homework log or journal for writing down homework assignments. Review it on a regular basis with your child.

Irritant 3: Your child daydreams and wastes time when doing homework.

Solution: Periodically check your child's homework to see how things are going. Give words of encouragement. Ask to see evidence of progress. Give your child a whistle to blow to let you know when he or she finishes the homework. Or allow him or her to set a timer to signal when to start and stop homework. Some experts advise parents to set a deadline for the completion of a child's homework. They insist that this will teach a child to take responsibility for getting the job done. Give privileges when homework is completed on time; deny privileges when it is not.

Irritant 4: Your child refuses to do homework; he or she does not feel like doing homework.

Solution: Plan on having a long discussion with your child, not a fight. Explain that you often do not like to go to work or make supper. But that is your job. When you perform it, it makes you feel good and proud. To get your child to do what he or she does not want to do, first acknowledge that your child has a right to such feelings. Then emphasize that homework is a job. He or she does not have to like it; but, as a student, your child is expected to do it. Stress that he or she will feel good and proud, too, when homework is completed. That is what your child's teacher, friends, and loved ones expect him or her to do. Also, consider using the incentives mentioned previously.

Note in the space below what has worked for you in dealing with any of the irritants above. Share these strategies with other parents.

Homework Tidbits

There are many suggestions on how to introduce your child to the specific subject areas of language arts, math, science, and social studies. These subjects form the core of a school's educational program. Some of the best advice for parents on this topic can be found in *The Parent's Homework Dictionary*, 2nd edition, by Dan J. McLaughlin. This dictionary gives definitions of terms from the above academic areas. It also offers descriptions and examples that are easy to understand. After reviewing this book, parents will have a stronger grasp of the subject matter that their child is studying.

Another book, *The Ultimate On-Line Homework Helper* by Marion Saltzman and Robert Pondiscio, presents a library of websites on a variety of school subjects. For families with a computer connected to the Internet, this is an excellent source of websites that parents and their children can explore together.

LEARNING EXPEDITERS

In every classroom, there are four major sources of learning. In a real sense, they are learning expediters; they accelerate the acquisition of knowledge. These are the teacher, textbooks, other students, and computers. Parents can help children learn how to deal with each one, thereby enhancing their performance in school. A starting point is for parents to understand the roles of these learning expediters in classroom instruction.

The Teacher

The teacher is in charge of instruction. What the teacher says or does has the most influence on classroom learning. Every teacher has a unique teaching style. This makes it difficult for a student to adjust to different teachers. Nonetheless, there are some general study practices your child can use with all teachers. Remind your child to do the following:

1. Always pay attention to what the teacher says and does.

2. Study what the teacher passes out in class (worksheets, study procedures, exercises, directions, etc.).

3. After viewing a film, filmstrip, or videotape, always write down what that presentation was about.

4. Look for teacher cues to what is important to know. Note especially when the teacher uses the following expressions:

    "This is important to remember."

    "This will be on your next test."

    "I want you to pay special attention to . . ."

    "Review this before you read the next chapter."

    "Knowing this will help you the most."

5. Take notes on what a teacher writes on the blackboard or posts on a bulletin board. These points are worth remembering.

6. Give special attention to what a teacher goes over several times.

7. Most teachers conduct review sessions over material studied. Be particularly alert at these times, noting areas stressed by the teacher.

Textbooks

A textbook is a book that covers a specific academic subject and is written for use in school. Textbooks teach. They are storehouses of information. They include many exercises to develop students' minds.

Textbooks are used widely in most classrooms. They are powerful learning tools. Many students fall behind in school because they never learn how to use their textbooks.

Parents need to know how textbooks are organized and how they present information. Once knowledgeable about textbooks, parents will be in a better position to help their children become comfortable with textbooks and get the most out of them.

Begin by taking time to examine your child's textbooks. Page through the book along with your child, stopping at the following sections and explaining them to your child.

A. **Common Elements**

Textbooks are generally organized in a similar manner and contain the following common elements:

1. Title Page—identifies title of the textbook and its author(s) and publisher.

2. Copyright Page—gives the date of publication and contains a copyright or ownership symbol ©.

3. Table of Contents—lists the contents of the textbook; it is an outline of a book, generally organized by chapters.

4. Preface/Introduction/Foreword—presents information on why the book was written and what it contains.

5. Supplementary Material (appendix, glossary, bibliography, index)—offers miscellaneous information: definitions of terms, references, and topics and names alphabetized for easy reference.

6. Chapters/Topics—represents major divisions of a textbook.

7. Illustrations—provides pictures, maps, graphs, tables, charts, cartoons, and the like, that illustrate the text and present interesting sidelights about a topic.

B. **Chapters**

Textbooks are subdivided into major sections, parts, or chapters. Chapters are the subdivisions found in most textbooks. Chapters deal with large topics or themes. Below is a typical organization of a chapter.

1. Chapter Title/Topic

2. Chapter Preview

3. Chapter Divisions/Sections/Subtopics/Headings

4. Chapter Illustrations (maps, tables, charts, graphs, etc.)

5. Chapter Activities

   ❖ Key words

   ❖ Key ideas

   ❖ Review questions

   ❖ Student activity/assignments

6. Chapter Paragraphs (first paragraph is the introduction; last paragraph is the summary)

C. Paragraphs

Within the chapters of textbooks are paragraphs. A paragraph is a group of sentences describing an idea, event, or subject. It introduces something new. Starting on a new line, a paragraph is indented or set off in some way to signal a change of thought.

Sentences and paragraphs are building blocks of information. They express the main ideas in the text and supply details supporting those main ideas.

Remind your child always to look for both the main ideas and details of the paragraph in each chapter. Every student should get into the habit of asking what the main ideas are in every paragraph. The answer can be written in the form of notes or jotted down in the margin of a textbook, workbook, or reader—provided students are allowed to write in these materials.

Understanding Chapters and Paragraphs

A parent can increase a child's understanding of textbook chapters and paragraphs by encouraging use of this simple formula:

1. READ IT—always on the lookout for main ideas.

2. WRITE IT—taking notes on main ideas.

3. TALK ABOUT IT—narrating these main ideas to oneself or someone else.

Urge your child to do several additional tasks to achieve mastery of a textbook:

1. Note which paragraphs are hardest to understand. These are the ones on which more time should be spent. Reread and study them thoroughly.

2. Note which pages or parts of a chapter can be skipped over. Often, the teacher will give clues on which parts are unimportant.

3. Devote extra time to completing the chapter exercises and activities designed for students. Even if they are not required by the teacher, doing them will expand student understanding of the chapter.

Remember: Children forget much of what they read; some say 50%, others 80%. To improve the ability to recall, parents can urge their child to do the following:

❖   Stop after reading a paragraph of a textbook and try to recall what was read; in particular, identify both the major ideas and the specific details.

❖   Practice recall by reading short, simple articles in a newspaper (or weekly reader in school) and explain what those articles are about.

❖   Write down the main idea of what they read or hear. Important details, concepts, and information stay with your child longer if they are written down. We tend to remember more what the brain translates into writing.

Parents also can improve their child's ability to recall by reading aloud a simple passage or paragraph, then pausing and asking the child to recall the main points.

The SSR Approach: Searching for Main Ideas

Being able to identify the main ideas in paragraphs or chapters is an important study skill for your child; you can do much to develop it at home. Review the following steps with your child. They are strongly recommended by learning experts. Advise your child to practice these steps daily in the classroom. When they become a habit, they will facilitate your child's learning.

1. Survey—Skim through all parts of a chapter before reading it closely. To survey is to take a quick walk through the material. The object of this first step is to give the student a general idea of what the chapter is about. The student need not read everything or read for details.

2. Study—Examine a chapter for details and specifics. This step is marked by a slow reading of material—taking notes if necessary, underlining or highlighting important points. Focus on what is important to know or remember.

3. Review—Review the chapter. Go over once more the important points to remember. Give special attention to the chapter's most important sections. Look for

    ❖   dates   ❖   people   ❖   processes/procedures
    ❖   events   ❖   ideas   ❖   causes/effects

Remember, try to make it a common practice to ask your child what the main ideas are in what he or she is reading or studying. Before long, your child will ask that question and will not need to rely on you.

To awaken your memory, what should you ask your child after he or she reads from a textbook?

_____

_____

Other Students

Other students are often overlooked as a source of learning. Students learn from each other. They need to know how to study with others, to work cooperatively toward common goals. Together, students can draw on each other's strengths.

Cooperative learning is a fresh change of pace. It can motivate students. It is also an effective means for generating information and stimulating study. Moreover, learning from others can be fun. As students grow older, they prefer to study with friends.

Some ways in which parents can encourage their children to work with other students are listed below. Parents can think of additional ways.

1. Structure a current events Saturday in your home, permitting your children to invite over selected classmates. Have them bring an item of interest for group discussion.

2. Encourage your child to invite certain classmates to your home for review sessions before a big examination.

3. Schedule a spelling bee at your home, with selected mothers and fathers managing it and selecting contestants.

4. Organize a "Special TV Movie Night" when a heralded educational TV program is scheduled (for example, the Civil War series, "The Computer Age," "The Age of Christopher Columbus," "New Wonders of Science," etc.). Supply popcorn and drinks. Review with the children key elements of the show.

5. Arrange a chocolate-chip cookie party with other parents at your house. After feasting, children are to ask each other questions dealing with what was learned in school the past week. The focus should be on specifics rather than generalities.

6. Host an occasional "homework night" at your home. Allow your child to invite several friends to study together on this evening. Establish several ground rules. They should include

    ❖ a quiet time, when complete silence is necessary

    ❖ a talking time, when children can interact

    ❖ time for demonstrating to you what was learned that evening

Provide treats for the children during breaktime. Be sure to give all children a warm goodbye when the homework is completed.

7.   Your suggestions?

_____

_____

_____

Computers

Another source of information students can draw on is the computer. The impact of computers on our nation and the world is staggering. We live in a computer culture. Computers are used virtually everywhere: in governments, banks, businesses, the military, and in medical and educational institutions. They have done more to revolutionize our lives than any other single technology. They will become even more important in your children's future. It is not a luxury for them to learn about computers. It is a necessity. That is why every state has mandated the teaching of computer literacy in schools.

Because children are exposed to computers early in school and get a chance to work on them regularly, parents should become at least marginally acquainted with this growing technology. Let's face it: children are sometimes way ahead of their parents in understanding computers. Words like mouse, keyboard, e-mail, word processing, and the Internet have become second nature to them.

Computers intimidate many parents. They fear that computers are too complicated to learn. This is not so. If children in kindergarten can learn about computers, so can parents. Parents should view computers as another tool teachers use to help students learn. Computers are like textbooks, overhead projectors, or blackboards, yet they have vastly more potential for student learning.

Do not be embarrassed if your children know more about computers than you do or if you cannot help them with their computer assignments. Just knowing about the basics of computers will be enough to show your children that you are interested in their work.

Many parents work with computers. They have them either at work or home; however, some parents have never touched a computer. The following information addresses both groups. It can serve as a review for computer-savvy parents or a brief introduction for those who are not.

What Is a Computer?

A computer is a machine linked together by wires, cables, and a multitude of parts. Computers do some of the things humans can do—only faster. They store huge amounts of information, solve problems, process commands, and retrieve data from all parts of the world. Moreover, they enable people to communicate with each other and engage in interactive activities. A computer reads information digitally with codes. Then it transfers such information electronically over phone or cable lines.

With computers, you are in charge; you tell them what to do. In the schools, computers are teaching devices and powerful tools for learning. Students use them to complete projects and conduct research. Computers help students connect to millions of bits of information, pictures, recordings, games, graphics, and other information sources.

In the October 4, 1999, issue of *USA Today,* Cindy Holland and Genevieve Lynn reported a study by NPD Online Research that discusses the linkage between homework and personal computers. The study stressed that children use a home personal computer for five main school activities:

1. Writing special reports.

2. Finding sources of reference.

3. Using software of an educational nature.

4. Doing homework at night.

5. Staying in contact with school friends.

Computers are more complicated than television or radio. You can turn on a radio or TV and change the channels or stations. This takes little learning. Moreover, you cannot tell them what to do. With computers, training is required. Once you understand computers, you are in command. Computers will respond to your orders.

Most of the 14,883 school districts in the United States have computers. A study conducted by the research firm Market Data Retrieval showed that there was a 105% increase in the number of computers found in classrooms around the country from the 1992–93 school year to 1998. In 1992–93, there were 3.6 million computers; there were 7.4 million in 1998. The study further reported that in 1998 there were 6.3 students for every computer. Tamara Henry summarized this study in the January 26, 1999, issue of *USA Today*. Try to find out the following information about your children's school:

1. What is the number of students per computer?

2. What is the model of computer being used?

3. How old are these computers?

4. What are their maintenance costs?

What Are the Main Parts of a Computer?

There are two components to every computer: hardware and software. Hardware refers to the network of cables, wires, and machinery. Among the main hardware is a monitor, keyboard, console, and mouse.

A monitor is a TV-screen-like unit that displays information.

A keyboard looks like the top of a typewriter. It is what you type on and use to send commands to the computer.

A console usually sits under the monitor or in a separate tower on the desk or floor. It is considered the most important part of your computer. It houses the "brain" of the computer. Data are stored in the console. This is where you insert the disks that contain computer programs, games, or other information.

A mouse is a small hand-held device connected to the computer by a coated wire. It has a left and right "clicker" (button) that enables the person using the computer to move the "pointer" (cursor) on the monitor screen in any direction. The cursor is a small symbol, often an arrow or vertical line, that tells you where you are on the computer monitor. The mouse is used to select information and programs on the monitor. When pointed and clicked, the mouse moves the cursor to select the display, icon, or program you want.

Software is what the computer depends on to work. It is programmed on round compact disks (CDs) or square floppy disks. These disks are inserted into a special opening on your computer's console. After software is "loaded" into the computer, you can use it to tell the computer to do the many things the program offers. Examples of software include Microsoft® Word and Excel.

What Do My Children Learn in School About Computers?

They learn the different components of a computer and how to turn it off and on. They learn how to use a mouse to navigate the screen, work with text, and select programs and functions. Children also practice using the keyboard and learn about how pressing certain keys will make the computer do certain things. They learn how to use a computer for word processing, which is like typing. Word processing allows you to move words and sentences around and change text more easily as you type reports or papers. Children learn how to use a printer to print out what they find or type on a computer.

Furthermore, children can also learn how to display graphics (pictures) and make charts, graphs, and tables. They can practice connecting to the Internet and finding information on the World Wide Web (www). Connecting to the Internet is referred to as going online. The Internet is often described as an "electronic highway" joining millions of computers from around the world. The World Wide Web is the graphic area of the Internet that includes websites. A website is a linked group of pages on one topic or for one company or organization.

On the Internet, students find many websites. There are websites for individuals, businesses, institutions, agencies, organizations, and other resources. They contain information much like magazines, books, encyclopedias, or newspapers. Children access these websites to find information about sports, medicine, newspapers, automobiles, fashion, products, statistics, school topics, and practically anything else you can think of.

In school, students learn how to use electronic mail (e-mail). Instead of sending a written letter via the post office, they learn to send a message electronically using the computer. Children also learn that they can get an e-mail address for themselves by signing up with an Internet Service Provider (ISP). Registration is also necessary to connect to and use the Internet. A fee is charged for this.

Furthermore, your children learn about the more popular Internet Service Providers like America Online, Prodigy, WorldNet, Earthlink, Microsoft's MSN, Juno, and MindSpring. There are many more local companies that provide access to the Internet. Internet Service Providers differ in fees charged for using their services, hours available for customer use, the speed with which they can connect the user to the Internet, and the degree of parental control over the content of online material.

How Can I Help My Children Improve Their Computer Skills?

Some ways are listed below. Perhaps you can think of other creative ways.

❖ Just as children can learn how to play a piano better if one is available to practice on at home, the same can be said for the computer. Purchase a computer for your home if you can afford one. Many computers are inexpensive. For parents who cannot buy a home computer, locate one at a nearby school, library, or church. Many of these sites allow the public to use their computers during certain hours. Escort your child to these sites several times a week for practice sessions. If possible, practice along with your child so you can become more knowledgeable about computers.

❖ Whenever you get the opportunity, such as during open houses or parent conferences, examine the software purchased by your schools. You will discover that there are software programs in reading, math, science, and other academic disciplines. Find out which ones are being used in your child's class. If you want to purchase a program for your child to use on your home computer, talk to his or her teacher about which ones are best.

❖ Talk to your children every day about what they learned on the computer in school. Encourage them to use computer terms in your discussion to develop their computer vocabulary. Invite them to help you look up the definitions of the terms that you do not understand.

❖ Schedule a conference with your child's computer teacher. Seek suggestions from him or her on what you can do to help your child enhance his or her computer skills. Teachers are an excellent source of ideas on this matter.

❖ Many bookstores and libraries have books or magazines describing the types of computer software available for home use. They evaluate the quality of software and determine which programs are parent and student friendly. Check them out.

❖ There is an electronic library on the Internet where students can find answers to research questions. This website is **www.elibrary.com.** Once you reach the website, type in the question or topic and click with your mouse on "go." The website will explain what your child has to do to conduct his or her research. This source has been around since 1995 and has served thousands of students. The user has to enroll in this program and pay a fee to use it.

There is another website that is a gold mine of information for youngsters struggling with their homework assignments. It contains information on certain subject matter and for various grade levels. There is no fee. The website is **www.refdesk.com.** Still another website that might interest parents is **www.edu-cyberpg.com.** Parents can connect to numerous educational resources that they can share with their children.

Get Computer Smart if You Are Not Already—Read!

Just as one size does not fit all, there is no one best book for parents interested in becoming computer smart. Literature on computers is found in libraries and stores in every community. Just search for it. The following two books explain in simple language the fundamentals about computers and merit reading by parents: Dan Gookin's *PCs for Dummies*, 7th edition, published in 1999, and *The PC Dads Guide to Becoming a Computer-Smart Parent* by Mark Ivey and Ralph Bond, published in 1999.

What Are the Main Complaints About Computers In or Out of School?

Some question the benefits of computer technology in schools. An ABC special television report on September 29, 1999, pointed out that the number of computers in schools has soared but student test scores have not. It acknowledged that several billion dollars have been spent on computer hardware and software for schools. Despite this enormous investment, student achievement has shown little improvement.

Many worry that more time spent on computers means students spend less time on reading and verbal interaction. In addition, many poor schools do not have the money to buy expensive software to operate their computers. Thus, they are at a disadvantage compared to affluent schools.

Another complaint relates to teachers. Some teachers seem to either fear computers or feel threatened by them. Or it may be that they are simply turned off by computers because they are not making the best use of this technology. Roughly one out of five teachers, as reported by ABC news in 1999, does not seriously incorporate the computer in his or her classroom.

Outside of school, students who have access to the Internet can access websites that display pornographic material. These websites are growing in number, hard to monitor, and often freely accessible to children. Parents are seeking ways to keep their children off these sites. Coming to their aid are government and Internet companies. They, too, are investigating how to block student access to websites that display or sell information that is inappropriate for children.

Parents should contact their Internet Service Provider for assistance. Many of these companies offer parent control features so children cannot access undesirable websites.

It is also possible for children to access material that promotes the agenda of hate groups as well as violence, the occult, bomb making, and other harmful topics. Some computer service businesses allow parents to filter or close such websites to children to protect them from this objectionable material. Parents should call their Internet Service Provider to find out how to do this.

Along another line, some websites collect information about children age 13 and under. Congress, mindful of this infringement on privacy, passed a law called the Children's Online Privacy Protection Act of 1998. In 1999, Congress enacted the final rules of this law. Starting in April 2000, companies must post on their websites the kind of information they collect on children and how this information will be used. Before websites post information on children or sell this information, they must get permission from the children's parents, either through a credit card number, e-mail, by phone, or in writing. These rules will gradually put parents in charge of the information gathered from their children.

Finally, children who spend time on the computer at school and then again when they come home are becoming physically lazy. They are not getting the exercise they need. Children can turn into "computer zombies" when they lose interest in other healthy activities for children their age. It is important for parents to limit their children's computer time, like their television time, so that fitness and social activities are not neglected.

REVIEW OF LEARNING EXPEDITERS

1. The four sources of information in the classroom are

   T _____

   T _____

   S _____

   C _____

2. The common elements of a textbook are

   _____

   _____

   _____

   _____

   _____

3. Identify one way you can motivate your child to study with other students in your house.

   _____

   _____

4. Discuss ways you can help your child develop computer skills.

_____

_____

_____

_____

Note-Taking Skills

PARENT STUDY GUIDE 5

FOCUS Taking notes and organizing information

PURPOSE Developing an understanding of note-taking in the classroom and organizing information

SKILL Guiding a child in learning several techniques for recording and organizing information

REFLECTION Sharing your thoughts, before and after this lesson, on improving your child's note-taking skills

Before:

After:

TAKING NOTES

FIVE PARENT GUIDELINES

Taking notes or writing down important ideas is a critical study skill. It is a skill that students need increasingly as they move through school. It should be taught in the early elementary grades. Students who learn how to take good notes tend to do well in school. Those who do not don't do as well. Some teachers spend time teaching note-taking. Most do not.

Information is less likely to be forgotten if it is written down. That is what taking notes means: writing down important things. Notes are nets that snare and store ideas. Taking notes is a talent parents can teach to help their children learn.

Note-taking takes practice. Practice may not make perfect, but it can lead to improvement. As with any skill, note-taking becomes easier through repetition.

If your children are too young to write, encourage them to take mental notes. They can do this by talking to themselves, repeating what they hear or see. If your children are old enough to write, they should be counseled to learn one of the many note-taking systems used by students.

Your child can use a tape recorder in class from which notes can be taken later on. Some educators frown on this practice. They think that it is too difficult to get information from the arduous chore of fast-forwarding or rewinding a tape. They argue that the process of taping is more time consuming than writing notes when instruction is going on. There are some schools, moreover, that forbid the use of tape recorders in class.

Note-taking is an individual exercise. Every child does it differently. For this reason, it is difficult for parents to assist their children in writing notes. However, there are five guidelines that parents can follow as they help their children acquire the knack of writing down information.

Parent Guideline 1: Stress how taking notes helps a student.

❖ Taking notes benefits students in several ways. First, it involves them directly in learning. Not only will they have to listen, they also will have to exercise their muscles and mind by writing down information they hear. The simple act of writing forces students to be alert, to pay attention, and to get involved.

❖ Second, when students take notes, they create a permanent record of important points that they read, hear, or observe. Writing down what is learned preserves it for reference later on.

❖ Third, taking notes permits one to recall big ideas and details. Forgetting occurs quickly after a book is read or a teacher is listened to. Taking notes allows a student to ensure that important information is not forgotten. It is a technique for memory enhancement.

❖ Last, note-taking teaches organizational skills. It teaches a logical process of collecting and storing information. These are skills that can be used in other walks of life.

Parent Guideline 2: Stress the role of notebooks.

Students need material on which to write notes. Just about any paper could serve this purpose. However, lined paper in a notebook is the best place to write notes. If a notebook is not affordable, loose-leaf paper, stapled together in book form, can substitute for a notebook. If possible, there should be a separate notebook kept for each subject—a science notebook, a social studies notebook, etc.

Parents should check a child's notebook periodically. See what kind of notes your child keeps, how neatly these notes are written, and if they make any sense. Go over the following reminders with your child. Follow up by checking a notebook for these points:

1. Clarity—Can notes be read and understood?

2. Completeness—Do notes cover a topic adequately?

3. Neatness—Are notes written with care?

4. Organization—Are notes organized in a systematic, logical, orderly way?

Parent Guideline 3: Stress the need for systematizing note-taking.

Good students do not just jot down notes in random fashion. They have a system for taking notes. A system is a plan that consists of parts working together so that a better job can be done. A carefully organized note-taking system has three parts: abbreviation, editing, and review.

Abbreviation

Note-taking is a kind of shorthand, a compression of language. It involves a condensed form of writing and recording. Notes summarize, outline, or digest.

When taking notes, your child should be reminded to abbreviate what is read or heard. He or she should not write down everything word for word. Nor should your child write in complete sentences.

Students should personalize note-taking. That means they should use their own words when they take notes. It also means that students should create their own code, symbols, markings, or abbreviations to speed up note-taking and save time. Here are several examples of abbreviated notes:

& = and	IM = important	? = question
St. = street	inf. = information	+ = add/increase
$ = money	♥ = love/charity	∫ = road, path, route

Notes should be written in a manner that is understood by the child. Encourage your child to consistently use the same shorthand language, one that makes sense to him or her.

Editing

Notes should be reviewed for editing as soon as possible after they are written down when the memory is still fresh. Editing refers to rewriting, clarifying, expanding, or smoothing out notes so that they are completely understood. This process enables the student to check his or her notes so that they make sense. This process also enables the student to clean up those notes that are hastily written or jotted down under pressure. In the editing phase, abbreviations can be spelled out, symbols interpreted, facts checked, inconsistencies corrected, and the outline tightened up.

When your child cannot make out his or her notes when editing them, advise him or her to ask the teacher for clarification. All teacher clarifications should be added to the notes. These clarifications should be placed where they belong in the outline of the child's notes.

Review

The third part of your child's note-taking system is review. Once notes are edited, they should be read once more. A review is more than a general survey. It is a close examination, intended to prepare the student for a test or class activity.

Your child will get more out of taking notes if he or she practices multiple reviews. The reviews should be done at least three times:

1. Immediately after notes are edited.

2. At the end of the week.

3. Before a test or class activity that relies on the notes.

Reviewing notes permits your child to understand more clearly how information fits together. It also helps your child to see the larger picture of what is studied. Make it a habit to remind your child to review notes in mathematics, social studies, science, language arts, and other subjects on a weekly basis. By doing this, you will enhance your child's learning in school.

To recall what you have just studied, list the three main parts to a note-taking system below:

A _____

E _____

R _____

Parent Guideline 4: Stress the importance of knowing common note-taking designs.

In school, children are expected to learn different kinds of information. They learn ideas, dates, events, people, places, causes, and effects. They also learn how to compare, analyze, evaluate, compose, question, and solve problems. What is studied usually determines the form of notes students should take.

There are many forms of note-taking. Note-taking instructors, however, emphasize several major designs. It is helpful for parents to know the following designs:

❖ Listing items.

❖ Writing notes in margins of a page.

❖ Underlining or highlighting key points of these designs.

❖ Mapping using diagrams and charts.

❖ Summarizing major ideas.

Each of these designs is illustrated in the chart on page 92.

NOTE-TAKING DESIGNS

Note-Taking	Information/Description	Examples
Design 1: Listing Items	Itemizing dates, battles, causes, effects, divisions, formulas, or other items that are best put in lists.	Topic: Beginning years of America's wars 1776—Revolutionary War 1812—War of 1812 1861—Civil War 1889—Spanish/American War 1917—World War I
Design 2: Writing Notes in Margin of Pages	This is used for pulling out the main points or ideas when reading a text.	Fire engines are found in all big cities. They save lives and property. Fire engines come in all sizes and shapes. Powerful machines, fire engines make a lot of noise. Their main purpose is to save lives and property. (These sentences can be reduced to words or phrases.)
Design 3: Underlining, Highlighting	Drawing lines under key ideas; placing stars, asterisks, etc., by points to know or remember; or coloring main points with highlighters.	The major <u>causes</u> of the <u>Civil War</u>.
Design 4: Mapping Using Diagrams and Charts	When knowing the relationships among items is important, students should draw tables, pictures, or diagrams of ideas, facts, or procedures. These "maps" show the relationship among items or ideas.	Composition of Congress House of Representatives (435) senators) | Senate (100) (each state has 2)
Design 5: Summarizing Major Ideas	This is done to condense information or to summarize what a teacher says or what is read.	**Summary** There are many forms of note-taking. The main ones are writing notes in margins, mapping, listing, highlighting, and summarizing.

OUTLINING

The most common form of note-taking is outlining. Widely practiced, outlining breaks down information into some kind of hierarchy, order, or pattern. Notes often are arranged this way to show the relationship among facts and ideas. Minor points are normally placed under big points. Large ideas are divided into smaller ones. Connections among information are highlighted.

Outlining is a popular note-taking technique for many reasons. The main ones are that it saves time and can be learned quickly.

One outlining strategy is to take a sheet of paper and divide it into thirds or halves. One part can be reserved for major ideas; another, for minor ideas or sub-points. A second outlining strategy employs columns and indented sections arranged in a descending order, such as the one below:

TOPIC

Date_____

Column 1   Column 2

    Main idea 1   —details

                                                     —details

    Main idea 2   —details

                                                     —details

    Main idea 3   —details

                                                     —details

    Main idea 4   —details

                                                     —details

As children get older, they can refine their outlining techniques. For all children, however, indenting serves a useful purpose. This is a way of setting off important points. It is also a way of showing how bits of knowledge are related and how they tie into major ideas. Examine the following example for organizing notes.

TOPIC: CIVIL WAR

Key Ideas

—worst war in nation's history

—showed a breakdown in the ability of North and South to compromise and work out a peaceful agreement

—divided country, then brought it back together again

Important Things to Study

1. Causes of War

    a.

    b.

    c.

2. Major Issues in the War

    a.

    b.

    c.

3. Lincoln and Lee

    a.

    b.

    c.

4. Critical Battles

    a.

    b.

    c.

5. Peace and Reconstruction

    a.

    b.

    c.

Parent exercise in outlining. One evening, watch an informative program. Listen carefully to what is said. Be alert for the major and minor points that are made. Outline them on this page. Be sure to date this sheet and abbreviate all the information you learn. Parents should compare notes with each other to see what they have learned.

TOPIC_____   DATE_____

Major Points	Minor Points
1.	a.
	b.
	c.
2.	a.
	b.
	c.
3.	a.
	b.
	c.

MAPPING

A relatively new approach to note-taking and retention is called mapping. It is a system that is consistent with how the brain works. The brain picks up and processes pictures, patterns, and vivid illustrations more quickly than just plain words. In mapping, students are urged to frame their notes in the form of diagrams, drawings, or sketches. Such mapping shows the larger picture. It also highlights the subject matter studied. This type of note-taking widens the ability of the student to recall and understand information. Parents should consider acquainting their children with this technique.

The four stages in mapping can easily be applied to note-taking. The first stage involves placing the main topic to be studied in the center of a page. The brain tends to zero in on what is in the middle. Our topic is oceans.

> Oceans

The second phase calls for adding main branches. These branches should extend from the main topic and represent important subtopics. Each branch should be drawn in a different color or differently shaped line and deal with a single subtopic.

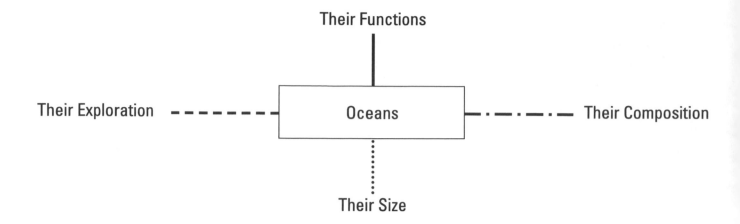

In the third phase, details are added to the branches. They can be connected by lines to the main branches (subtopics). These lines present expanded information about the subtopics. Lines also can be drawn from these "twigs," adding even more details to these smaller topics.

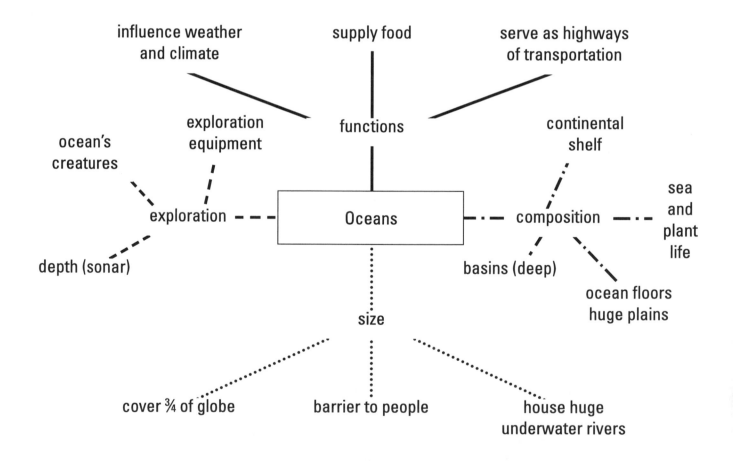

The last phase in mapping deals with personalizing information. Here is where students create their very own symbols, signs, codes, or shorthand that aids them in recalling information or seeing relationships. A student, for instance, may want to compose an acronym or mnemonic device like $FESCO_4$ to trigger recall of information on oceans. Or the student may draw symbols representing specific events, ideas, or concepts.

FESCO4 stands for the topic of Oceans (The main topic is represented by the larger letter). Four aspects of oceans to remember are their functions (F), exploration (E), size (S), and composition (C).

Parent Guideline 5: Stress the need to know teacher cues.

Because knowledge grows every day, teachers are increasing the volume of learning, and they expect students to keep pace. They also expect students to distinguish the important from the trivial. In this effort, parents can help out. A good place to start is understanding where students acquire information and ideas.

Generally, students learn from two sources. These are instructional materials (books, worksheets, audio-visual aids, computers, etc.) and the teacher. Taking notes from the former is easier. This is because students can regulate the speed of these sources. Since students can start and stop these sources, they have more time to jot down important points.

Taking notes from teachers is another matter. It is more difficult. Some teachers talk fast; others are difficult to follow. Thus, trying to decide what to write down and remember from teacher presentations becomes a taxing chore for many students. Since teachers are the chief source of notes in classroom learning, students need to know how to handle teacher talk.

The first step in learning how to take notes from teachers is by being a keen listener and an alert observer. Parents can help their children get more out of teacher talk by sensitizing their children to cues from the teacher. Prep your child to take notes on certain things a teacher does:

1. Giving definitions.

2. Making comparisons.

3. Listing items.

4. Presenting key words, drawings, or ideas.

5. Emphasizing certain points. In particular, listen for the phrases:
    "This is important."
    "You will see this again."
    "This will be on the test."
    "Study especially this material."
    "Remember this."

6. Giving illustrations (telling a story, showing a film or transparency, displaying an object or map, passing out a diagram).

7. Posing questions (especially review questions).

8. Emphasizing learning objectives.

Parent Guideline 6: Stress the importance of taking notes from reading.

Students commonly obtain information for papers, projects, and tests from reading materials like books, magazines, newspapers, encyclopedias, almanacs, and World Wide Web pages. It is easiest for most students to use the outlining approach discussed earlier when they take notes on these readings.

Suggest that your child jot down notes on all reading material that answers the questions:

Who?   What?   When?   Where?   Why?   How?

Students should not write complete sentences on the answers to these questions—just a word or short phrase that can speed recall. If your child finds an inspirational, moving, or powerful idea, fact, or statement, it can be copied word for word with quotation marks around it. Be sure your child writes down the source of the quotation.

Note taking is a shortcut to learning. It helps students remember important information. It highlights the specific persons, places, things, or ideas your children are expected to learn in school. Remind your children that, after reviewing notes taken from readings or in class, they should make it a habit to close their eyes and visualize these notes. Tell them, also, that quietly repeating notes to themselves can place them more deeply in their memory.

REVIEW AND DISCUSSION FOR PARENTS

There are five parent guidelines to follow in strengthening your child's note-taking abilities. See if you can restate them. If you cannot, page back to where they are discussed and copy them below.

Parent Guideline 1

Parent Guideline 2

Parent Guideline 3

Parent Guideline 4

Parent Guideline 5

Parent Guideline 6

Preparing for Tests

PARENT STUDY GUIDE 6

FOCUS   Preparing for tests in the classroom

PURPOSE   Becoming familiar with strategies for helping a child prepare for tests

SKILL   Helping a child prepare for tests

REFLECTION   Sharing your thoughts, before and after this lesson, on your child's test and testing procedures

Before:

After:

TESTS AND EXAMINATIONS

THE PROS AND CONS OF TAKING TESTS

Tests and examinations are an important part of school. Like most things in life, they have a good and bad side. On the good side, they measure how much a student understands about a subject. They give us an idea of how well a child is learning. On the bad side, tests trigger anxiety and fear. All too often, they are the reason why children dislike school.

Taking tests involves two processes. One is studying to prepare for the test. The other is taking the test itself. Test preparation takes more time, and some think it is the harder of the two. Taking a test, on the other hand, tends to be more stressful. It can create anxiety and forgetfulness.

When you were in school, remember how you felt about tests? Tests meant clammy hands and heart palpitations. They turned you into a bundle of nerves. Well, your children have similar feelings. Mentioning tests to them sets in motion an avalanche of nervous feelings.

Your Feelings About Tests

Illustrate in the space below how you felt about tests when you were in school. Express these feelings in any form: lines, pictures, images, colors, symbols, words, etc. Then try to analyze your final product. Use the same exercise with your child. This activity allows you and your child to discuss the anxieties these feelings create. It also shows whether you have negative, neutral, or positive feelings about tests.

How I Feel About Tests

Tests are not monsters. They have no fangs. They need not be feared. Parents can decrease their children's panic and improve their performance on tests by helping them understand that tests are a normal part of school.

Becoming "Test Smart"

To begin, tests should be portrayed as student-friendly. Their overall purpose is to help students. Tests strive to find out how much students have learned. Parents should try to convince children that the best way to deal with tests is knowing how to prepare for them and become "test smart."

There are several approaches for teaching your child to become test smart. None is better than having a conversation on tests with your child. Talking about tests can do much to demystify them. Start by discussing with your child what tests are and how they present opportunities for the learner. You can base your comments on the material below.

1. **What are tests?**

    Tests are a series of questions on subject matter studied. They determine how much a student has learned about a topic or subject. Everyone who goes to school takes tests. Instead of sources of anxiety, tests can be windows of opportunity.

2. **How are tests opportunities for a student?**

    Tests give students a chance to show how much they know, how much they have learned, and what they need to work on to become a better student. It is important to remind students that they can learn from taking tests and from test results. Tests are like games. Some children are not good at games. The reason is because they have not learned to play the game right.

    It is the same with tests. Students who are not good at taking tests normally have not prepared themselves properly to take tests. Tests challenge participants. Students can rise to the challenge merely by learning the game. Tests, like games, can be fun.

PREPARING FOR TESTS

You have just explained tests to your child as games where participants prepare to do their very best because they love the challenge involved. Focus on test preparation as the key to performing well. Emphasize this point again and again. Explain to your child the following reasons for preparing for tests:

1. To take the fear out of tests.

2. To do well on tests; to get good grades.

3. To avoid panic and stress.

4. To find out how much a student has learned or failed to learn (identify areas for improvement).

Next instruct your child to prepare for a test by going over the following points. Remind your child to

1. Attend classes consistently. Be present. Be in school.

2. Always read the textbook and class material before a class discussion on the material.

3. Take notes on class instruction and textbook reading. When taking notes, highlight important points. For example, draw a single line under big ideas and a double line under details, put stars beside items that have special importance, or use different colors to highlight the most important and least important points.

4. Study notes before a test; pay attention to the following:

   ❖ Know definitions of terms and concepts.

   ❖ Know itemized lists (three of this and four of that).

   ❖ Know categories, classifications, elements, and parts.

   ❖ Review points emphasized in class.

   ❖ Review areas that the teacher asked you to study.

   ❖ Review material that the teacher wrote on the blackboard or passed out in class.

   ❖ Review questions in study guides and questions at the end of textbook chapters.

5. Urge your child to ask the teacher what percentage of the questions for the test will be taken

   ___1. From the textbook?

   ___2. From related reading material (workbooks, outside reading, etc.)?

   ___3. From notes?

   ___4. From other sources?

   Then spend proportionate study time on these materials. For example, if three fourths of the test will be taken from the textbook, three fourths of your child's study time should be spent on reviewing the textbook. Or, if one half of the test will cover classroom notes, then one half of a child's test preparation should be devoted to studying the notes.

TAKING TESTS

Once again, preparing for tests is the best way to deal with them; and preparation takes time. Persuade your child to allocate sufficient time to study for a test. Time is the key to test preparation. Impress on your child that it is a student's responsibility to find time in his or her daily life to get ready for a test. Your child's preparation routine should include rereading and writing. Encourage your child to read and write down information that will be covered by examinations.

Reread material for main ideas and details. This aids retention. The more the material is reread, the easier it can be recalled.

Write down key ideas, terms, and definitions. This is an excellent rehearsal for a test. When you put information in writing, you draw a picture or image of it. It sticks with you longer.

Advise your child to anticipate what will be on the test. Test material will come from chapters or sections of a textbook or workbook; from teacher-student discussion; from what the teacher writes on the blackboard or passes out in the form of worksheets, written exercises, or miscellaneous handouts; and from teacher cues such as the following:

"This will be on the test."

"I expect you to know this."

"You will see this material again."

"This is of special importance."

"One third of this material will show up once more."

Frequently, students do not set aside enough time to prepare for a test. They "cram" the day before a test. The brain simply cannot sort out information jammed into it in a short period of time. Cramming is the worst way to study for a test. It is far better to begin studying for a test days in advance.

Marcia J. Coman and Kathy L. Heavers, authors of the 1999 book, *Improve Your Study Skills*, suggest that students review test material four to six days before an examination. They prescribe the following routine:

On the first night:	Quickly read through the material.
On the second night:	Skim again; review your notes; read aloud key points to yourself; try listening to the important points as you say them.
On the third night:	Reread notes and study material one more time; say aloud to yourself what they mean to you.

On the fourth night:	Compose a sample test; take it and check how well you have done. If you did great, do not go any further; you are ready.
On the fifth/sixth night:	If you did not do well on the fourth night, review your material and take a sample test (given to you by a friend or parent). Do this on the fifth night and, if needed, a sixth night.

PARENTS AS TEST ENGINEERS

Engineers are trained to skillfully direct a building project. In like fashion, parents can be trained to be engineers of their child's test-preparation efforts.

As a test engineer, your job is to build your child's understanding of what it takes to prepare themselves for tests. Be sure your child receives the following before a test:

❖ A quiet place to study.

❖ Adequate rest.

❖ A nutritious meal.

❖ A complimentary, reassuring word, such as "Good luck on your test," "Give it your best shot," "I know you'll do great," or "Show them how much you know."

Remind your children that when they take the test, they should do the following:

1. Breathe deeply and slowly several times and make their arms and legs go limp to relax.

2. Look over the entire test before answering any questions. Skimming over a test before beginning gives students a large picture of what is on the test.

3. Read carefully all directions to be sure what is asked for.

4. Watch the clock so they have a chance to complete all the questions.

5. Budget their time carefully.

6. Not worry about finishing first.

7. Stay away from students who bother them, and avoid all noise and distractions.

8. Have pens, pencils, and eraser on hand before taking the test.

9. Work first on the easy questions.

10. Code difficult questions (place an **X** by these questions, circle their number, or jot a question mark next to them). Skip them and return to them later.

11. Proofread answers before turning in the test.

The most important point you can make is to stress the importance of starting to study early for a test. Do not wait until the last moment. It is best to start studying for a test a week ahead so that test material can be reviewed thoroughly.

To help children do this, parents can do two things. First, persuade children to keep a color-coded test folder for each subject in school. Children should take responsibility for decorating it and making it attractive. All tests and papers for that subject should be stored in these folders for future reference. When a comprehensive examination on that subject is scheduled, parents can direct their child to review the material in the folder.

Second, with the help of the child, parents should construct a "Do Not Disturb: Preparing for Test" sign. This sign should be stationed by the child when he or she is studying for a test. It gives special attention to this type of activity. Together, parent and child can dress up this sign with colorful graphics and catchy phrases. An example of one is: "Mind in gear. Test is near. Don't bother the dear!" Make the sign large enough to be visible from a distance.

Ground Rules for Tests

Parents should coach their children to ask their teachers the following six basic questions about tests. These questions can serve as ground rules for tests. When children know these answers beforehand, they will be in a better position to handle items on a test.

1. How much time will students have to take a test?

2. Do all questions on the test have to be answered?

3. Will students be penalized for not answering a question?

4. Can the answers be written in ink or pencil?

5. Do test questions have to be answered in any order?

6. What kind of test will be given?

Of all these ground rules, the last is the most important for students preparing for a test. Students should always know the test format. It determines how they should study for the test.

KINDS OF TESTS

There are two major kinds of written tests that are given by teachers. These are objective tests and essay tests or a combination of both.

Objective Test

This is a test that either presents answers that students have to identify or requires a brief written response. Studying for this type of test generally requires remembering details. In fact, objective tests rely on recall and memorization of details. Objective tests come in several forms.

They are described below with their chief features. Parents are advised to discuss this information with their children so that they become familiar with these tests.

1. **True-and-False Tests**

   ❖ These tests are presented in sentence or statement form.

   ❖ All parts of a statement must be true to make it true.

   ❖ If any part of a statement is false, the entire statement is false.

   ❖ Look for words like never, only, always, none; they tend to make a statement false.

   ❖ Do not read too much into the statement; your first response is usually the best one to use.

2. **Multiple-Choice Tests**

   ❖ This test presents a number of answers (three to five) after the question or statement. Students are asked to pick the right or best one.

   ❖ It is important for a child to read carefully each of the possible right answers.

   ❖ If a child cannot make a decision, urge him or her to place a "?" by that item and return to it later.

3. **Matching-Items Tests**

   ❖ Like the multiple-choice test, a matching-items test presents a number of answers. They are usually arranged in two columns. Students must link or match items that go together.

4. **Completion/Short-Answer Tests**

   ❖ These tests require a word or a short sentence to complete the answer.

   ❖ Short-answer tests often call for opinions and analysis, as well as facts and details.

Essay Test

Another major kind of test is the long-answer or essay test. This test allows students to put together their own responses using sentences and paragraphs. It requires skill in writing and organizing information. Essay tests develop thinking skills by requiring students to analyze, compare, describe, interpret, evaluate, or synthesize.

Facts and details are important in essay writing, but how they are organized is even more important. That is why many test experts advise students to outline their essay answer in advance. An outline enables a student to organize his or her answer before writing it.

When preparing for essay tests, children should be reminded to

1. Know what is wanted in the essay question. Look at the action verb; highlight it with a circle, asterisk, star, or other symbol. If the verb is *discuss, analyze, explain, describe,* or *interpret,* then do that.

2. Open the essay with an introduction, telling what you propose to do and how you will present your ideas.

3. Organize the body of your answers in a systematic, logical way, such as:

    Big Idea 1
      details, facts, examples

    Big Idea 2
      details, facts, examples

    Big Idea 3
      details, facts, examples

4. Try to show relationships between people, events, and items; compare and contrast; identify patterns.

5. Write an answer employing key terms or words used in the textbook or in teacher discussions. Also use good grammar and proper sentence structure.

6. Close an essay with a conclusion. A conclusion reviews and summarizes the main points.

TEST-MAKERS

Parents need to know that another way of viewing tests is in terms of their authorship. Regarding authorship, tests fall into these categories:

❖ Teacher-prepared tests are designed by classroom teachers themselves. These tests reflect the materials and skills that are deemed important and taught by your child's classroom teacher.

❖ Commercially prepared tests are composed by companies that write or publish instructional materials for the schools (textbooks, workbooks, and supplementary works). Many teachers use the tests that accompany student textbooks.

❖ Standardized tests are written by testing companies that establish national norms and administer the same test to large groups of students. These tests may be given statewide, to a specific region, or across the nation.

Now that you have completed this lesson on preparing children for tests, move to the next page. Jot down specific ways to help your child become test smart over the next week. To jog your memory, review this module.

PARENT ASSISTANCE: PREPARING FOR EXAMINATIONS

THIS WEEK I WILL take the following steps
to help my child prepare for examinations:

_____
(Child)

MONDAY

TUESDAY

WEDNESDAY

THURSDAY

FRIDAY

Memory and Thinking Skills

PARENT STUDY GUIDE 7A

FOCUS   Teaching memory improvement at home

PURPOSE   Examining techniques for improving one's memory

SKILL   Acquainting a child with useful memory enhancement devices

REFLECTION   Sharing your thoughts, before and after this lesson, on strengthening your child's ability to remember

Before:

After:

PARENT STUDY GUIDE 7B

FOCUS   Teaching thinking skills at home

PURPOSE   Familiarizing parents with thinking and problem-solving skills adapted for home use

SKILL   Stimulating a child's thinking skills

REFLECTION Sharing your thoughts, before and after this lesson, on parents teaching children thinking processes in the home

Before:

After:

MEMORY ENHANCEMENT

The ability to recall information and experiences is based on a person's memory. Memory is the part of the mind that reconstructs what has been heard, seen, learned, or lived through in the past. A good memory improves one's chances of doing well in school.

While some are born with strong memory skills, others have to cultivate them through concentration and hard work. Students can learn to improve their memory with help from their parents. A place to begin is by understanding some of the dynamics of retention. Once parents understand this phenomenon, they can practice with their children specific strategies for memory enhancement.

WHAT PARENTS NEED TO KNOW ABOUT MEMORY

A good memory will certainly aid students in their schoolwork. Sometimes, memory is viewed as mental impressions that are slowly forgotten. Memory is the opposite of forgetting. Both have been subjects of study for years.

Some believe that students never forget what they learn. Throughout life, every bit of information absorbed is stored in the brain, waiting to be recalled when needed. If we cannot remember something, it is because either it was never properly stored or we have not found a way to spark its return. The good thing about memory is that it can be improved through practice.

Students can increase their memory in several ways. They can start by knowing when forgetting takes place. Once this is known, students can take steps to remove these memory blockers.

Forgetting for most students occurs

❖   immediately after something is learned

❖   when learning is not graphic, colorful, useful, or fun

❖   when information is not written down or repeated to oneself

❖   when information is not periodically reviewed

❖   when information is not used, practiced, or applied

Parents can help their children "groove their memory channels" by preventing the above barriers from interfering with their ability to recall. Review the following strategies. Practice them with your children. To work, these strategies must be repeated often.

STRATEGIES FOR MEMORY ENHANCEMENT

1. Use direct personal experience.

Memory is heightened by direct personal experience. When students vote, march in a band, visit a museum, walk through a mock-up of a human heart, or sit in a cockpit of an airplane, they tend to remember these experiences for a long time. Students also will recall more easily what they have learned if they have had to apply it. So encourage your child to use what he or she has learned. Firsthand experience and direct application of what is learned in the classroom tend to be remembered.

2. Spotlight important ideas.

Parents should insist that their children always look for important ideas in their classes. Children can be taught at home to separate the important from the unimportant. Those things labeled as important will stay with children much longer. Parents should fall into the habit of asking their children what was the most important idea learned in math class, science class, etc. Get in the habit of asking your child what was the most important idea in a book that he or she read or TV show he or she viewed.

3. Self-talk.

What children need to remember should be recited out loud. Talking to oneself, going over important information, can drive this information deeply into one's memory bank, where it can be drawn on later. A child should practice self-discussion, mulling over information at frequent intervals. It will be recalled more easily when needed later.

4. Write things down.

One of the best ways to stamp information into our memory is by writing it down. This preserves it for retrieval later on. Encourage your child to write down what is important to remember. Then, check frequently to see if your child does this.

Permit your child to write things down that you want to remember: grocery lists, a to-do list for next week, addresses of friends and family, and the names of people to invite to birthday parties, showers, or weddings.

5. Practice, drill, repetition.

Three shortcuts to learning are practice, drill, and repetition. All three carve paths into one's memory. To learn something well, a child should go over it numerous times. Repetition is a great teacher and a surefire way to long-term retention. Find out from your child some things that have to be remembered in each subject. Then help your child drill this material. Time needs to be set aside to do this. Examples of parent-run drills are found on the next page:

❖ How much is 9 x 9? Give me some division problems you studied in math.

❖ Can you tell me again the three results of your lab experiment?

❖ Once more, recite the causes of the Revolutionary War.

❖ Describe the two effects of environmental pollution covered in your science class yesterday.

❖ Repeat the two ways mountains and hills are alike and the two ways in which they are different.

6. Overlearn.

Overlearning is learning more than is necessary at that time. Keep in mind that children tend to overlearn what they like or enjoy. Parents should understand that time spent in overlearning material promotes recall of it. Children should review material even after it has been learned. Not only does overlearning make recall automatic; it also breeds confidence in knowing material well. One overlearns through practice, drill, repetition, and review.

Why do people remember how to drive a car after a long layoff? One reason is because they learned this skill exceptionally well. It comes back to them quickly when it is needed.

Or why do people remember phone numbers, anniversary dates, birthdays, and other facts? One explanation is that they learned such details through practice or through repeated use. Another reason is that they just made it a point to master this information.

7. React to what is read, heard, or seen.

Your children should try to remember to ask three questions when studying their subjects. Answering these questions will help them remember the material. These questions are:

What? _____

Why? _____

How? _____

If your children can answer these questions in class, they will certainly be on the way to expanding their memory skills.

8. Visualize.

Another memory technique is visualization. This is forming a mental picture of what is to be remembered. This is an excellent way to help young children recall things. Encourage your child to close his or her eyes and then create a picture of what is to be remembered. The child should give it color, enlarge it, and dwell on it for a few moments.

9. Play the "Reminder Bag" game.

On occasion, parents can strengthen their child's memory skills by playing games. Try this one. Take a grocery bag, box, or folder and decorate it with pictures that your child likes (CDs, candy, toys, sports, pizza, dolls, heroes). Instruct your child to write daily on small pieces of paper things that they do not want to forget: phone numbers, important dates, facts learned in school, addresses, etc. Then direct the child to drop these notes into the "Reminder Bag" (or "Reminder Box"or "Reminder Folder"). Later on, urge your child to play the Reminder Bag Game by asking your child, "What was deposited today in your Reminder Bag?"

10. Use memory exercises.

One's capacity to remember grows with exercise. Teach your child to do the following mental calisthenics. They will stretch his or her memory capabilities. Challenge your child to memorize

- ❖ street signs
- ❖ baseball cards
- ❖ license plate numbers
- ❖ telephone numbers of friends and family
- ❖ batting averages
- ❖ details in the shopping mall
- ❖ Saturday TV shows
- ❖ books read in previous grades
- ❖ names of all past teachers
- ❖ the first 10 presidents
- ❖ all the teams in the NFL
- ❖ the eight longest rivers in the world
- ❖ the planets

11. Play the home game.

You can play this game at home with your children. It will not only bolster their memory skills, but it will also improve their listening and concentration skills. At least once a week, ask your children to verbally repeat what you say to them. Make a game out of this. Make your phrase simple at first but increase its complexity over time. Then have them write what you say in a complete sentence. A complete sentence has the following elements:

A subject—the person, place, or thing about which something is said.

A verb—the word showing action or state of being (i.e., is, am, was, be, etc.).

Finally, a sentence must make sense. It must stand by itself. Have your children draw a picture of the subject that you talked about. You may have mentioned taking out the garbage, cleaning their rooms, writing a letter to grandma, or going to church. You select the topic. Let your children share their work with each other.

THINKING AND PROBLEM SOLVING

Both thinking skills and memory skills are important. Memory is the recall of past information. Thinking is processing information, particularly using it to deal with new situations. Thinking is oriented to the present and future.

Knowing how to think is a skill that can serve a child throughout his or her life. That is why thinking skills have long been a prime objective of education. In recent years, there has been an increase of interest in this topic. It is felt that the ability to think is the best preparation for a student to meet the challenges of an increasingly complex world.

The brain is like a muscle. Thinking stretches it. It enlarges one's intellect to deal with the world. Thinking is more than memory or factual recall. It is organizing, interpreting, questioning, and evaluating. It is figuring things out.

Thinking tends to be more difficult than memorizing. It requires additional energy and effort. All learning is about thinking. In the end, good study habits facilitate thinking.

Many parents shy away from teaching their children how to think for themselves. They feel that it is too difficult for them to do this. On the contrary! In small ways, every parent is capable of developing a child's thinking powers. Parents should steer their children to become thinkers at an early age. The earlier a child is challenged to reason things out at home, the easier it will be to expand this skill in school.

To prepare to teach thinking skills, parents first should acquire knowledge on this topic, including the following ideas:

1. Schools teach students how to think.

2. Thinking is more than just memory; though complex, it can be learned.

3. Thinking can be defined in a number of ways; simply, it refers to the ability to reason, to figure things out, to solve problems.

4. Teachers use a wide variety of strategies to teach thinking. These include

   ❖ asking higher order questions (how or why?)

   ❖ teaching how to form and test hypotheses (a theory or guess stated to be proven)

   ❖ teaching concept analysis (a word or words that categorize objects, ideas, feelings, and other life experiences)

❖ allowing students to find things out for themselves (discovery)

❖ allowing students to come up with their own solutions and creations

❖ using deductive and inductive reasoning techniques

❖ requiring students to use the scientific method in their studies

❖ employing the steps of problem-solving

To repeat, parents can help teachers develop a child's thinking skills by efforts they make at home. Learning thinking skills needs to start in the home and should continue throughout a child's school years. Parents play the main role in preparing their children for the rigors of learning thinking skills.

There are three ways in which parents can fulfill this role. First, create an environment at home that encourages your children to "stick their neck out," to question and challenge. Keep in mind, there is risk in small people searching for answers in a world of giants (adults). Questioning may be interpreted as rebellious behavior. Besides challenging authority, a child's inquisitiveness may be viewed as disrespectful.

Although such behavior may make people feel uncomfortable, parents should encourage it. Children need to know that their parents stand behind them when they seek answers. They need to know that there is nothing wrong in using one's wits or arguing a point of view. If parents support their children at home in the use of critical inquiry, these children will be more inclined to exercise it in school.

A second way parents can beef up their children's thinking skills is by serving them a heavy diet of experiences that require the use of higher-level thought processes.

Children cannot think in a vacuum. They need experiences on which to reflect. As noted earlier, it is a parent's obligation to enrich their children's lives by taking them to zoos, museums, libraries, shopping malls, and on vacations. Furthermore, parents should try to surround their children with puzzles, books, calendars, posters, science fiction, riddles, stories, current events, and news programs. These experiences are the basis for reflective thought.

Riddles are excellent intellectual exercises. A riddle is a mystery that provokes thinking. It calls for a solution or answer that requires serious reflection. Parents should purchase, or check out from the library, a book of riddles to use with their children. Riddles are fun. They can be used with both young and older children.

Identify a riddle that fascinated you the most. Share it with your child. See if he or she can solve it! Give him or her clues if necessary.

Here is an example of a time-worn mystery: "The Riddle of the Sphinx." What has four feet in the morning, two in the afternoon, and three in the evening? The answer is Man. As a baby (morning), he crawls. As an adult (afternoon), he walks on two feet. As an old man (evening), he needs a cane or third foot. Write your favorite riddle in the space below.

My Favorite Riddle

THINKING SKILLS

There are many kinds of thinking skills. They have been classified by notable scholars. Parents can lend a hand in teaching these skills at home. All ignite a child's creativity, arouse curiosity, and stretch the intellect. Examining them separately makes it easier to understand them. Several thinking skills are listed below along with parent-led activities to promote these skills.

Higher-Level Thinking Skills	What Parents Can Do to Encourage These Skills
1. INTERPRETING means explaining or showing what something means.	Cut out graphs, charts, tables, etc., from a newspaper or magazine. Ask your child to interpret the graphic. Give a prize for the effort.
2. EXPLAINING means making something clear and understandable.	Inquire how things compare and contrast (are alike and are different).
3. EVALUATING means judging, arguing, or estimating; expressing an opinion.	Routinely ask your child's opinion on a subject or topic.
4. PREDICTING means foretelling or declaring beforehand; making a prediction.	Ask your child what he or she feels is going to happen.
5. OBSERVING means watching, paying attention to, or noticing.	On a trip, ask your child to explain what he or she sees or notices.
6. ANALYZING means studying in detail; determining the evidence; breaking down a subject, separating the parts, and examining their relationship to each other.	Frequently inquire of your child how parts or elements of something studied fit together.
7. CLASSIFYING means grouping into sections or categories; sorting or placing into classes.	Ask your child to tell you into what groups certain items should be placed or arranged.
8. SYNTHESIZING means pulling together; assembling into a whole; solving, planning, proposing, or constructing.	Ask your child what he or she learned from a specific experience or school project.
9. COMPREHENDING means describing or grasping; understanding; comparing and contrasting; explaining in one's own words.	Ask your child what the author, speaker, presenter, teacher, or friend meant by what he or she said or did.
10. HYPOTHESIZING means assuming something for the sake of an argument; proposing a theory, explaining something.	Present this scene to your child: "What if you did . . . ? What do you think would happen?"
11. MENTAL TRACKING OUT LOUD means talking to oneself.	Push your child to recite what he or she is mentally going through in figuring out an answer or problem. Reciting experiences help to vitalize thought processes. Say, "Tell me what you were thinking and how you arrived at that."

Asking "Why" Questions

Another strategy for stimulating your child's thinking is to ask "why" questions. The following are samples of why questions. Can you think of others?

SAMPLE WHY QUESTIONS

- ❖ Why is grass green?
- ❖ Why do people die?
- ❖ Why are aircraft carriers so big?
- ❖ Why do some animals have fur?
- ❖ Why do children have to go to school?
- ❖ Why do students need to study before tests?

What are some why questions you can ask your children? Normally, children ask adults these questions. Turnabout is fair play. Parents asking why questions can arouse curiosity and trigger higher-order thinking in their children.

To motivate your children to think, draw the shape of a balloon on a piece of paper. Write the questions above in the middle of the balloon. Ask your child to rise to new heights by searching for answers to these questions. Make a habit of occasionally dropping these questions on your child's bed, dresser, or desk. Offer a reward or special privilege for answers to these questions.

PROBLEM-SOLVING SKILLS

Parents can increase their children's thinking ability by teaching them to solve problems. Although there are many specific thinking skills (comparing, analyzing, inferring, evaluating, generalizing, and the like), solving problems is a very important one. It is the skill that most characterizes good thinkers. Moreover, it is a thought process that can serve your children in all their classes. And it is a skill that they can apply in their future experiences.

Parents should encourage their child to practice problem-solving techniques in dealing with problems in their home or community. After all, genius lies in solving the problems of everyday life, according to an expert on thinking skills, Edward de Bono.

Problems that can challenge children in the home are

- ❖ resolving who takes out the garbage

- ❖ settling an argument between a brother and sister

- ❖ deciding what to do about dirty alleys or polluted dumps nearby

- ❖ deciding how to deal with gangs in the neighborhood

- ❖ finding ways to stretch the family budget to cover upcoming expenses

Parents can improve their children's thinking skills by giving them specific family problems to solve. They also need to help their children learn the steps of problem solving. And they need to present children with frequent opportunities to practice these steps.

Problem-Solving Process

Parents can use the problem-solving format below at home to prepare their children for problem solving in school.

Steps	Sample Problem
1. Identify problem. ❖ Be aware. ❖ Use careful observation. ❖ Spell out details of the problem.	1. Insufficient weekly family allowance for spending. ❖ There's not enough money to meet weekly expenses. ❖ Lack of funds creates a hardship for me (the child). ❖ I can't afford to do what I want to do.
2. Collect information on problem. ❖ Set up plan for acquiring data, statistics, facts, etc. ❖ Set up system for storing and retrieving information.	2. Find out the amount of allowances given to children in other families. ❖ Research topic of family allowances and other information that bears on this case. ❖ Organize this information in a folder and label it.
3. Interpret the information. ❖ What does it mean? ❖ What does it show or prove? ❖ Give explanations. ❖ Identify relationships and patterns.	3. An analysis of the data shows that my allowance is the highest in the neighborhood. ❖ Data shows that the last time my allowance was increased was 2 years ago; other kids received an increase 6 months ago. ❖ Data shows fewer kids are receiving weekly allowances. Cost of living is up; things cost more today.
4. Brainstorm list of possible solutions. ❖ Come up with as many solutions as possible without evaluating them.	4. There's more than one way to solve the problem: a. Increase my weekly allowance. b. Lower my expenses (buy less). c. Write my dad's boss and request he be given a raise. d. Drop the allowance altogether. e. Work at persuading my older brother to contribute to my weekly allowance.
5. Evaluate the above solutions. ❖ What are the pros and cons? ❖ Who is helped or hurt?	5. Some solutions are better than others: a. If given, this would mean more work and responsibility. b. Possible, but will force me to do without some pleasures. c. Long-shot; may anger the boss against my dad. d. Would set a bad example, and what would I live on? e. Reasonable option, since a few pennies wouldn't hurt him. They would help me.
6. Make a decision. ❖ Present arguments for it. ❖ Defend it as the best of all the possible solutions.	6. Lower my expenses. Prioritize my needs, from most to least urgent. Then eliminate those items I can live without. This decision will cause the least amount of hardship to the allowance receiver and allowance giver.

To teach your child problem-solving skills, parents themselves must be able to model them. Review the six steps on the previous page. Walk your children through these steps. Then discuss some problems that exist in the home or neighborhood. Together, write these problem topics in the subsequent table. Urge your child to practice the steps of problem solving in handling these problems.

Possible Problem Topics in the Home	Possible Problem Topics in the Neighborhood
1. _____	1. _____
2. _____	2. _____
3. _____	3. _____
4. _____	4. _____

THE PMI METHOD

Another way to foster critical thought is to use Edward de Bono's "PMI" method. PMI stands for "Pluses, Minuses, and Interesting Points." This is a systematic method for examining life's problems. Its purpose is to teach students to be broadminded, to see all sides of a problem. Students are urged to explore what is good (plus) about a decision or situation, then what is bad (minus) about that decision or situation. Finally, students describe what is merely interesting about the situation.

To illustrate: Faced with the prospects of closing school for the rest of the year, a child may think about this situation using PMI.

PLUSES	MINUSES	INTERESTING POINTS
❖ More free time	❖ Can't see my friends	❖ Reactions of parents
❖ Can do what I want to	❖ Can't play ball or cheerlead	❖ More people in the streets
❖ Can sleep late in the morning	❖ Won't get an education	❖ The impact on the community
❖ Can get a job and make money	❖ Too much time on my hands	❖ What happens to tax money marked for schools?
❖ Others?	❖ Others?	❖ Others?

Parents can create a number of similar scenarios, such as the ones listed below, and train their child to practice using the PMI method.

- ❖ Should homework be abolished?

- ❖ All stores should be closed on Christmas Eve.

- ❖ Allowances for kids should be tied to the cost of living.

- ❖ Would it be a good idea to do away with grades in school?

Such thought-provoking, mini-lessons at home could include these questions or themes. Use the format below.

PLUSES	MINUSES	INTERESTING POINTS

TEACHING ANALOGIES

Edith Bernhardt, in her 1988 book *ABC's of Thinking with Caldecott Books*, presents a thinking strategy for developing reading skills. She stresses the use of analogies. An analogy is a comparison or likeness of items that have some things in common. The words as and like are used in analogies. She cites these examples:

Shoe is to foot as mitten is to hand.
Nose is to smell as ear is to hear.

Parents can make up similar examples for their children. Besides teaching the concept of analogies, these exercises will stimulate their thinking skills. You can use the following examples with your children. See if they can come up with the answers.

1. Boat is to water as airplane is to_____(sky).

2. Church is to pray as playground is to_____(play).

3. Dogs are to barking as lions are to _____(roaring).

4. Head is for thinking as heart is for_____(feeling).

5. Teaching is for teachers as learning is for_____(students).

6. Rockets are to science as paintings are to_____(art).

7. Jogging is to exercise like reading is to_____(learning).

8. Sailor is to navy like soldier is to_____(army).

9. Girl is to female like boy is to_____(male).

10. Libraries are to books like banks are to_____(money).

Write several analogies yourself and share them with each other.

_____

_____

Ask your children to come up with a few analogies of their own.

_____

_____

TEACHING SYNONYMS AND ANTONYMS

Another way of looking at words is through synonyms and antonyms. Synonyms and antonyms can be found in a book called a thesaurus. Synonyms are words that are similar. Antonyms are words that have opposite meanings.

The words sleep, doze, and nap are **synonyms**; they mean the same thing.
The word pairs smile/frown and run/stand are **antonyms**; they are opposites.

Work on these two forms of word pairing with your children at home to make them think and expand their word skills. The beauty of these exercises is that they need not take a lot of time. You can practice them at mealtime or while driving in the car.

Have your children find a word's **synonyms** (similar or comparable words). Remember that there might be many words, not just two, that have the same meaning. Encourage children to write their own synonyms and note them below.

sprint	_____ (dart)	_____	_____
walk	_____ (hike)	_____	_____
affectionate	_____ (loving)	_____	_____
work	_____ (labor)	_____	_____
automobiles	_____ (cars)	_____	_____
shoe	_____ (slipper)	_____	_____

Also, press your children to find a word's **antonyms** (opposites). Keep in mind that there might be many words, not just two, that have opposite meanings. Encourage your child to write his or her own antonyms and note them below.

happy	_____ (sad)	_____	_____
love	_____ (hate)	_____	_____
difficult	_____ (easy)	_____	_____
adult	_____ (child)	_____	_____
big	_____ (small)	_____	_____
beautiful	_____ (ugly)	_____	_____

REVIEW

This unit explains to parents ways of teaching their children memory and thinking skills. Both are tools to help children increase their brainpower. These skills do not develop overnight. Nor do they grow on their own. They take time to develop; they need to be practiced.

There is no best way to teach these skills. Parents will have to experiment, trying different techniques and devising challenging games. What seems to work should be used again and shared with other parents.

Parents can turn the home into a memory and thinking center in two ways:

Learn more about memory development and thinking enhancement.

Spend time with their children while applying techniques to improve memory and thinking skills.

Reading Skills

PARENT STUDY GUIDE 8

FOCUS   Improving a child's reading skills

PURPOSE   Learning how to become a reading facilitator

SKILL   Teaching a child techniques for reading improvement

REFLECTION Sharing your thoughts, before and after this lesson, on how you can become a reading facilitator

Before:

After:

PARENTS AS HOME READING TEACHERS

THE NATURE OF READING

Children will never excel in school unless they can read well. Of all the skills necessary for school success, none is more vital than reading. Will Rogers once remarked that a person learns in two ways. One is reading; the other is associating with smarter people. Notice that he ranked reading first.

Reading is the cornerstone of learning. That is why so much time in school is spent on teaching reading. Good readers tend to make good students.

Too many children cannot read well; and even more prefer to do things other than read. One study, *Turning Points: Preparing American Youth for the 21st Century,* pointed out that only 11% of 13-year-olds read adequately. One need only ask teachers to find out that a large percentage of students do not enjoy reading.

Parents should realize that reading is the skill most commonly used in school. About 80% of schoolwork involves reading. Therefore, if a child cannot read well, he or she will struggle in all subjects.

Many elementary school teachers devote more than half of their instructional time to building the reading skills of their students. Toward this goal, they use a wide variety of materials and techniques. They work in small reading groups or one-on-one with students. Teachers can do a more effective job teaching reading if their efforts are reinforced at home.

Not all educators want parents to teach reading. They contend that this requires specialized training, which parents do not have. When trying to teach reading skills to children at home, they argue, parents may interfere with what the experienced reading teacher is doing in school. These critics also feel that parents may inadvertently place undue pressure on children in pushing them to read.

Despite these reservations, parents cannot be ignored in the so-called reading improvement crusade. Their involvement can make the difference in raising the reading level of students throughout the country. Parents can do a lot about a child's attitude toward reading. Attitude is where parents can play the biggest role.

How children view reading depends largely on their parents. Children's feelings toward reading are shaped well before they enter school. Parents, primarily, do the shaping in the home. Even when children are in school, parents play a major role in their reading attitudes.

Parents do not have to be experts in reading to influence their children's reading habits. They do need to have some knowledge of reading. More specifically, parents need to know how reading is taught in the school and how to use time at home to prepare their children for formal reading instruction in school. In this way, parents can become reading facilitators. Regardless of their educational background, all parents can assume this role. A facilitator is one who makes things easier for another. A facilitator works directly with another, tutoring and encouraging. Take a few minutes to read the following poem by Mary Beth Stanley. What does it tell you about a facilitator's role?

A POEM TO PARENTS

All of you are parents
But you're also teachers, too
And if you want to help your child
I'll tell you what to do.

Whenever you're in the kitchen
Let your child be your helping hands
And show them all the labels
And let them read the brands.

Say beginning and ending sounds
And find some things that rhyme
And they will quickly learn to read
In a short amount of time.

Let your children help you measure
The butter, eggs and flour
And let them help you set the timer
For thirty minutes or an hour.

Then, when you have to leave your house
In the car or for a walk
Don't forget this is another time
To teach and learn and talk.

Read all the street signs that you pass
And the house numbers by the door
And all the license plates on cars
And there is so much more.

There are many words on buildings
And trucks and cars you meet
There are billboards standing tall
And shops on every street.

Then when at last you do return
And you sit down together
Please take this opportunity to read
A book about whatever.

Being a parent is very special
But as a teacher you are special, too
Just take the time to make learning fun
And your child will love what you do.

In their role as reading facilitators, parents should do two things. First, show a love for books and the written word. You should make a habit of reading. Try also to supply your home with a wealth of reading material: travel literature, newspapers, magazines, library books, calendars, catalogs, store flyers, and advertisements. Much of this literature is free. Let your children frequently see you with reading material in your hands. Above all, talk to children about the wonderful world of books.

The following statement on the magic of books by the late author Louis L'Amour gives parents a barrel of ideas from which to draw when they talk about reading to their children. Review it several times. Underline points worth sharing with your children.

The book has been man's greatest triumph. Seated in my library, I live in a time machine. In an instant I can be transmitted to any era, any part of the world, even to outer space.

I have lived in every period of history. I have listened to Buddha speak, marched with Alexander, sailed with the Vikings, ridden in canoes with the Polynesians. I have been at the courts of Queen Elizabeth and Louis XVI; I have been a friend to Captain Nemo and have sailed with Captain Bligh on the Bounty. I have walked in the agora with Socrates and Plato, and listened to Jesus deliver the Sermon on the Mount.

Best of all, I can do it all again, at any moment. The books are there. I have only to reach up to the shelves and take them down to relive the moments I have loved.

—*The Sackett Companion* (1992)

A second way parents can function as reading facilitators is by interacting with children in the home and engaging them in the use of words. Reading to children is the key. It should start early and be done with regularity when children are young.

THREE INTERVENTIONS TO FACILITATE READING

To be able to function as reading facilitators at home, experts say that parents need to intervene in three major ways: early reading stimulation, word identification and reading approaches, and reading comprehension. When practiced repeatedly, these parent interventions will go a long way in helping a child learn to read well.

Early Reading Stimulation

Right after birth, infants are capable of learning. They respond to sounds, words, and other forms of stimulation. Infancy is not too early to prepare them for reading. Many reading experts argue that by the time children enter first grade, their reading aptitude has been formed. Thus, what parents do with their children during their preschool years is critical. Parents are in a choice position to lay a strong reading foundation for their children on which teachers can build. Do the best you can to turn your home into a language-rich environment.

Examine the widely circulated chart below and its language development suggestions for young children. Infants and toddlers are especially responsive to certain parent activities. Parents should practice these activities in short intervals and integrate them into a daily routine.

Age Groups	Parents' Activities
Infants	Talk to them, read to them, sing to them.
8–9 months	Recite nursery rhymes, lullabies, fables, and short stories.
12–14 months	Show pictures and urge children to talk about them.
1½–2 years	Read stories and recite poetry, allowing toddlers to turn pages, ask questions, and express feelings.

Parents are the chief agents in preparing their child for reading. Preparations for reading should start in a child's infancy. All the reading research advises parents to read to their children as they grow up. Children learn to read from hearing their parents read.

Word Identification and Reading Approaches

Children learn to read by identifying words. The more words they know, the better they will read. Today, a debate rages among educators over the best way to teach reading. Some vote for phonics; others, for a more natural approach. Most reading teachers say that children should be taught to identify words and learn to read using several approaches.

One approach promotes sounding out letters or a combination of letters (syllables) in a word. This is called the "phonics approach." Phonics is learning letters and words through their sound. While some words are not spelled the way they sound (c can be a soft or hard letter; k is silent in some words), sounding out letters and words when learning how to read does work with many children. After practicing letter and syllable sounds, students learn to decode words. Decoding is figuring out what a word means. It is unlocking the meaning of a word.

Another way to identify words or learn to read is through the "look and say approach," sometimes called the "sight approach." Children are shown picture cards with the name of the word below. The idea here is to have a child see the whole word, how letters are arranged in the word, and how the word is spelled. Once visually grasped, the child is encouraged to say or recite the word. Hopefully, a child will then remember the appearance of this word, in effect learning the word. He or she will soon learn not only how to say the word but also what it means.

A third way of teaching reading is by emphasizing whole language. This approach has the support of many reading teachers. According to this approach, children should be allowed to read or figure out words naturally, on their own. Children will understand the meaning of words by their association with words they already know or by the context in which the words are used. Whole-language advocates insist that children learn to read by reading. They also argue for teaching reading and writing together, naturally.

A fourth way to teach reading is called the "balanced approach." It is presently being used by increasing numbers of elementary school teachers. This approach utilizes whole language, phonics, and practices that veteran teachers have found work best for them. So the balanced approach draws on what teachers see as the strengths of each method of teaching reading and identifying words.

The publisher Houghton Mifflin has simplified the procedure for both teachers and parents in helping children study a word. This procedure outlines the steps parents can follow in working with their children at home to learn words.

HOW TO STUDY A WORD

Step 1. LOOK at the word.

Step 2. SAY the word.

Step 3. THINK about the word:

- ❖ Sounds like?
- ❖ Any related words?
- ❖ Is there a pattern?

Step 4. WRITE the word.

Step 5. CHECK the spelling.

Reading Comprehension

A third way parents can function as reading facilitators is by helping improve their child's reading comprehension. Comprehension has become a chief focus in reading instruction today.

There are many levels of comprehension. In general, comprehension means understanding what is read. Specifically, it means being able to identify main ideas and details in a passage.

Many children fall into two traps when it comes to reading comprehension. One is the trap of spacing out, where the mind wanders and daydreams, making it impossible to pay attention. Such inattention leads to poor comprehension of what is read. The other trap is a poor vocabulary. When students cannot recognize words, they will find it difficult to understand reading material.

Teachers everywhere are constantly working to improve reading comprehension. They teach spelling, structural analysis of words (root words and syllables), and vocabulary development.

There are almost one-half million words in the English language, in addition to 300,000 technical words. The average person knows fewer than 5,000 words; children know even fewer. Since learning new words is critical to reading comprehension, teachers could use help from the home. Spelling and vocabulary development are cornerstones of reading comprehension. Teachers, primarily in the early grades, spend a lot of time on spelling. They use workbooks, flashcards, a list of words mandated for each grade level by the schools or the state, and even words selected from reading material studied in class. Consider the following question.

Remember how you learned to spell in school? Discuss with each other the best way you learned to spell.

Typically, the best readers tend to be the best spellers. So it makes sense for parents to help their children learn how to spell. Here is an idea. Every other day, identify a word that you find in your reading or conversation. Bring this word to the attention of your children. Spell the word and have them write it on a small sheet of paper. Post it somewhere in their room. Casually refer to this word and expect your children to spell it verbally. Start with simple words, slowly graduating to harder ones. Their rooms should be "wallpapered" with words in no time. Before long the home will have the reputation of being a rich "word library" for children.

Most teachers assign spelling words to students. Insist that your children bring home this list so you can see it. Then be sure to go over these words with them. Always ask your children to use words verbally in a sentence. This will help them increase retention of these words.

In addition to spelling, vocabulary development is critical to reading comprehension. Like spelling, vocabulary development is the business of the home.

Parents can enlarge their child's vocabulary in a number of ways. The more words your child understands, the greater his or her reading comprehension. The secret is to get a child excited about learning new words and understanding what is read. A few exercises you can use with your child at home are provided on the following pages.

1. Ask your child to repeat at least five new words he or she heard on TV in the past week. You can help your child spell the word. But let him or her look up the definition and try to use the word in a sentence.

2. Ask your child to bring home a word he or she did not understand in class and discuss it with the family.

3. Encourage your child to complete simple crossword puzzles. Give your child a hand, if necessary.

4. Urge your child to quietly craft questions on what is read—namely, higher-level questions: why? how? what if . . . ? Questions on reading material force children to examine more deeply what they read, leading to greater comprehension.

5. Whatever a child reads, reminding him or her to ask certain questions about the reading will increase comprehension. These questions are:

    ❖ What was the story/passage/chapter/book about?

    ❖ What did you not understand about the reading?

    ❖ What was the most interesting part of the reading?

    ❖ What was the most boring part of the reading?

    ❖ What do you think you will remember most from the reading?

6. Encourage your child to read ads in newspapers (ads about food, clothes, furniture, autos, toys, records), looking for new words.

7. Challenge your child to discuss what he or she reads. Discussion promotes deeper understanding of material.

8. Help your child build a book bin or book shelf where he or she can store reading material.

9. Insist that your children read to you the warning labels on cans, bottles, and boxes in the home, showing you they understand these warnings that may save their lives.

10. Work with your child in preparing a "Home Vocabulary Scrapbook" for the school year. Words that are new or fascinating should be entered by your child in the scrapbook. Suggest that your child write definitions of these words. Let your child design the cover and decorate the inside.

11. Encourage your child to read labels on soup cans, cereal boxes, cookies, bread, and packages.

12. Ask your child to draw an object or picture of new words. Some words can be easily pictured (like *domicile* or *continent);* others will be more challenging (like *century* or *beauty).*

13. Tape-record your child reading aloud; play the tape back and pick out words your child is not sure about or words he or she would like to learn more about.

14. Start singing to your children when they are infants. Continue this practice as they grow. Childen will memorize words and sing along with you. Singing expands their vocabulary. It increases their word comprehension, too.

15. Encourage your child to think through new words. Sometimes the meaning of the word can be figured out by how it fits in the paragraph. Reading comprehension can come from connecting words, using the known words to decipher the new one.

16. Provide opportunities for your child to sound out words, to identify what letters are blended together.

17. Help your child learn how to analyze words by reducing them to their syllables. Words can also be better understood by breaking them into their roots, prefixes, and suffixes. Some examples are given here. Can you think of other words that can be broken down this way?

    a. Root—main part of a word
        examples: *port* (carry) and *connect* (link, join)

    b. Prefix—letters added to the beginning of a word
        examples: *de*-port (remove) and *inter*-connect (connect between or among)

    c. Suffix—letters added to the end of a word
        examples: *port-able* (able to be carried) and connect-*ion* (noun: tie, bond, linkage)

18. Play word-rhyme games with your child. Think of words that rhyme with certain words: house, home, charity, etc.

19. Always provide your children with a dictionary suitable for their age. Keep it near them when they read. Suggest that your children look up all words that they do not know. Assist them in using the dictionary.

20. Talk your child into using new words learned in conversation with others, not to show off but to make these words a part of his or her vocabulary.

21. Persuade your child to use recently learned words at home and in writing assignments in school.

22. Install a "tough word" spelling board in your child's room. When the child learns to spell a difficult word, he or she can "publicize" it on the board. This board can be made from a

cardboard box and decorated by your child. Tell him or her that you are going to boast about this board when others visit the home. Display your pride for your child to see.

A generous display of workbooks containing lessons for teaching reading can be found in bookstores, teacher stores, discount stores, and drugstores. Children are invited to trace over letters, connect dots to form the shape of letters and words, color syllables and letters, and add letters (*-ed, mis-, -ion, -ing, re-*) to change the meaning of words. Parents can examine these workbooks for ideas to teach reading comprehension at home.

Time to Review

So far, this module has identified three ways in which parents can become reading facilitators. Can you recall what they are? If not, look back through the chapter to find them. Then write them on the following lines.

1. E_____ R_____ S_____

2. W_____ I_____ and R_____ A_____

3. R_____ C_____

STUDENT COMPREHENSION NOTEBOOK

You can help your children improve reading comprehension by encouraging them to keep a "comprehension notebook" for each subject. They can use the following format. Once children become accustomed to this format, it will not take too much time.

While writers present different kinds of information to readers, they organize their ideas in certain patterns. The main ones are listed below. As students read a textbook, they should decide whether the writer's purpose is to

1. describe (people, events, issues, procedures, crises, problems, etc.)

2. compare and contrast

3. list, itemize

4. show time sequences

5. indicate cause and effect

These categories can be explained easily by parents. Give examples of each category. You can take examples from newspapers or textbooks that your child brings home. Point out passages that describe, compare, list items, show time sequence, or indicate cause and effect.

Help your child complete the following form the first few times. Then let your child work on his or her own. Periodically, check the work. Be sure to show interest in efforts to increase reading comprehension.

COMPREHENSION NOTEBOOK FORM

Subject _____

Text _____

Chapter/Page _____

1. Describe

2. Compare and Contrast

3. List, Itemize

4. Time Sequence

5. Cause and Effect

Encourage your child to complete this form after completing each reading assignment in all of his or her subject areas. Pages can be stapled into a notebook. This notebook can serve as a convenient aid for review and test-taking.

KNOW YOUR CHILD'S READING AND STUDY HABITS

Children have different reading habits. Some read fast; others, slow. Some understand what they read; others find it hard to comprehend reading material. Some remember what they read; others struggle with recall.

Before parents can help a child with study habits, they have to know his or her reading habits and learning style. You can gain insight into your child's reading habits by responding to the questions below. Share your findings with your child.

READING AND STUDY HABITS

Does my child . . .

Quickly settle down to work or take a long time to settle down to read?	
Have a relaxed or stiff posture when reading or studying?	
Tend to study or read in the morning/afternoon/evening?	
Have nervous habits that are visible while reading?	
Reading habits: ❖ Use fingers to point at words? ❖ Move his or her lips as he or she reads? ❖ Reread passages? ❖ Have difficulty understanding passages? ❖ Forget what was read?	
Daydream a lot or stay focused on schoolwork?	
Hurry through work/take time/be careful about schoolwork?	
Have to snack when studying, when reading?	
Get upset when disturbed while reading or studying?	
Talk about what is read to ❖ parents? ❖ brother? ❖ sister? ❖ friend? ❖ no one?	

READING SPEED

Parents need to know if their child is a good reader. Scores of reading experts highlight these characteristics of a good reader.

A good reader

❖ remembers what is read

❖ understands what is read

❖ reads at a smooth, rapid rate

How fast a child reads depends on four factors:

1. Eye training.

2. Knowledge of words (vocabulary).

3. Difficulty of reading material.

4. Practice in reading.

With elementary school-age children, reading speed is not stressed; comprehension is. It is difficult to establish reading speed rates for children in every age group. Most teachers would rather focus on helping every child determine his or her own speed to ensure comprehension of what is read. Reading speed is tied to purpose. If the purpose of reading is entertainment, one's reading pace tends to speed up. If the purpose is understanding, reading speed normally slows down.

Everyone can improve reading speed. There are certain benefits from being able to read fast. The most obvious one is that more can be read. A less obvious one is that reading becomes smoother, a more natural activity. Reading speed is improved through practice. When reading becomes a daily habit, reading speed will increase. The best way parents can help their children become fast readers is by making sure they read every day.

Some time ago, the Association of American Publishers released some rough measures of reading speeds. The average reader tends to read 250 to 350 words per minute (WPM) of easy material; 200 to 250 WPM of average difficulty, and 100 to 150 WPM of difficult material. These are figures for adult readers. Most young children do not read as fast as adults. If you want to know the average reading speed of children in your child's grade, consult his or her teacher.

SILENT VERSUS ORAL READING

In practicing to become strong readers, children should have the opportunity to learn how to read silently and aloud. Both have advantages. Silent reading disciplines a child to become an independent reader. It also can lead to deeper understanding of the printed word. When reading alone, one can pace the reading, speeding up and slowing down as one chooses. Not having to pronounce words has certain benefits. It allows the reader to read faster and cover more material. It also does not tire a person as much as reading aloud. The older the child becomes, the more he or she should rely on silent reading.

Oral reading also has advantages. It is especially helpful for beginning readers or slow readers. Understanding for them can be enhanced through recitation. Just as important is sharing with others what was read, its wonders and fascination. Reading aloud permits the listener to evaluate a child's reading habits. In addition, it serves as a tool to diagnose problems. Many experts suggest that a child be given time first to read over material before reading it aloud. Allow your child to do this before you request that he or she read to you.

MOTIVATING CHILDREN TO READ

It has commonly been said that there are three "enemies" of reading. All are found in the home. Some have been mentioned before. They are noise, television, and parents who fail to read. Fortunately, these are problems that parents can do something about. Parents can share with each other their ideas or strategies for combatting these enemies. Jot down the strategies that you think will work in your own home. Once these foes are dealt with, parents can work on exciting their children about reading.

Combatting the Enemies of Reading in the Home

Noise Strategies:	Television Strategies:	Parents Not Reading Strategies:

Listed below are some suggestions for motivating your child to become a good reader. Review them and discuss them with family and friends. Then use these ideas in your home.

1. Make sure your child has good vision. An eye exam is the best way to ensure good vision. Glasses should be worn to correct vision problems. If a child cannot see well, he or she will fall behind in reading development.

2. Provide some quiet time during the day for reading. It is the parent's job to arrange the home to promote reading. What is needed most is silence and a place for reading. Weave reading time into your child's daily schedule.

3. Tell stories. Everyone loves stories. Make them up if necessary. Include in your stories interesting characters, plots, and endings. Story-telling is excellent preparation for reading. Stories introduce children to reading symbols, sounds, and values. Always allow preschoolers to talk about the stories that they hear. This develops language skills.

4. Enroll your child in a story-hour sponsored by your church, library, school, or community agencies. Meeting with other children who are also interested in reading is a strong motivation for reading. Story-hour programs dramatize reading and portray it as a fun activity.

5. Play word games with your child. Show your child words and help him or her pronounce these words. Encourage your child to identify words that sound the same or have syllables that sound the same. Give prizes for using words in a sentence or telling stories using new words.

6. Set up a home library. Stock it with newspapers, magazines, pamphlets, and paperbacks acquired from the library or bought at garage sales. A library environment at home does much to enhance the magic of books.

7. Make it a habit to read in front of your child. Show him or her that reading is an important part of your life. Be an example that your child can emulate. Display a large appetite for the printed word. Make it clear to your child that you get immense joy from reading.

8. Read to your child. Not only does this draw child and parent closer together, but it also increases the child's enthusiasm for the world of books. Start reading to your child when he or she is an infant.

9. When reading to your child, pronounce words slowly, be dramatic, be expressive, raise your voice, show emotions, and exaggerate. Reading to older children presents opportunities to point out letters, syllables, words, and pictures. Afterwards, discuss these matters with your child; play on his or her natural curiosity.

10. Take your child to the library as soon as he or she is old enough for a library card. Make sure you have one, too. Check out books for yourself. Then allow your child to select books for reading. Remember: set an example.

   Many libraries have book sale rooms where books are donated and sold at exceptionally low prices. You can purchase a handful of books for a dollar or two. Find out the hours and days when the used book sale room is open in your neighborhood. Browse through the collection of materials with your children. Allow your children to pick out the books they would like to read.

11. Guide your child in making a reading place mat on which to eat. On the place mat should be printed an inspirational, upbeat message about the importance of reading. Help your child come up with one. When done, this place mat will be a constant reminder to the child of the importance of reading.

12. Talk to your children about what they read. All children find reading more fun if they have a chance to talk about it with others. Talking also increases their comprehension of what is read.

Do you know how much your children read and the kind of reading material they prefer? Write your answers to these questions in the box below.

PARENT-CHILD WORD ACTIVITIES

Do these exercises with your children over a 2- or 3-month period. Urge them to find the words requested. You can make a large poster for these exercises to place in your child's room. Give a prize or special privilege to your child for completing these word exercises. On occasion, replace the words below with new words to challenge your children.

Word Exercises

1. Find words that rhyme with the following:

dollar	dime	cool	boat	tax	tub

2. Place words in the following categories or groups:

planets	vegetables	cities	flowers	colors	sports	animals

3. Find words that match the required number of letters:

2-letter words	3-letter words	4-letter words	5-letter words	6-letter words	7-letter words

Remember, Parents:
Show a love of reading by working with your children to become better readers.

A FINAL WORD

Congratulations, you have finished a lengthy journey. Along the way, you have been armed with skills to boost your child's performance in school. The trip took two paths. One led to developing stronger study habits in your child. The second pointed the way to reinvigorating your family by drawing parents and children closer together.

Never before has there been as much concern about children and the family. Numerous government studies and advocacy groups have stirred up interest in the plight of America's children. These efforts have led to an abundance of programs for saving the American family. In spite of these good intentions, this cherished American institution continues to slip.

Parents today spend only 17 hours per week with their children, 40% less than in 1965, according to a 1994 University of Maryland study. The following year, a Gallup Poll found that nearly half of all parents feel that they spend too little time with their children. Fewer than one-third of these respondents ate dinner together on a regular basis. These studies are cited in the 1996 book, *Family Time: What Parents Want,* published by the Family Research Council in Washington, D.C. This trend seems to demonstrate that children are fast becoming unimportant in the lives of their parents.

Furthermore, teachers everywhere are frustrated about teaching children who refuse to learn. Their frustrations are similar to that of a physician treating a patient who refuses to take the medicine that will save his life.

The following is a lament of another teacher. She is disappointed by the inability of young children to handle the simplest learning tasks in kindergarten.

> I have observed children coming into kindergarten with little or no academic or behavior skills. Many can't pay attention or follow rules. Some children have never picked up a crayon, pair of scissors, or paint brush. Some children switch hands when they write, color, or trace. They never develop a dominant hand in writing and they get very confused. Others clench pencils and crayons as if they were holding a pop can. They also have no feel for spatial relations. I have seen children use scissors like hedge clippers, using both hands. Moreover, language, visual discrimination, visual memory, and social skills are seriously deficient. Children do not understand what words mean.

This observation corresponds with the findings of many national studies. In the report, *Ready to Learn: A Mandate for the Nation,* published by the Carnegie Foundation for the Advancement of Teaching, Ernest L. Boyer discusses a survey of 7,000 kindergarten teachers. These teachers felt that 35% of children entering school are not adequately prepared to do schoolwork. According to many kindergarten teachers, this lack of preparation is getting worse, not better, among children entering school. Typical teacher comments were that children cannot name colors, identify where they live, or recite their complete name.

Given this gloomy situation, the tendency is to fix blame. But pointing fingers of blame will not solve the problem of poor student learning. Nor will promises and noble intentions. Action by parents will. This has been the message resounding throughout this manual.

Studies have shown that preschoolers and kindergarten children possess an infectious enthusiasm for learning. They are excited about life and school. Yet as they grow older and move through school, they lose this zest. Most disturbing is that they do not perform up to their potential in class. The drop in interest in school is due to many factors: lukewarm teachers, peer pressure, irrelevant or dull learning material, poor facilities, and unsupportive homes.

It is up to parents to ensure that their children do not lose this gusto for learning. If their children are grounded in strong study skills, it is likely that they will remain enthusiastic. Sylvia Rimm identifies 12 laws of student achievement in her 1996 book, *Why Bright Kids Get Poor Grades: And What You Can Do About It.* The most compelling law is this: When parents become effective models of behavior, children will imitate them. Student achievement depends on parent achievement, especially parental attitudes toward achievement.

Parents are being asked to help schools improve learning for America's children. This is education's grand quest. All the talk about school reform or improving student learning is meaningless without massive parent participation. Make no mistake: the home is the command center for student learning. Parent initiatives can promote good study habits. All told, if children were asked to vote for the one person who can help them do better in school, they would cast ballots for their mom or dad.

PASS hammers on the theme: Parents can make a difference. Since children tend to imitate their parents, parents need to be a model for their children, one that displays a love for learning, the value in a good education, and skill in studying. Above all, PASS urges parents to make themselves available to children during their schoolwork, to help them use their minds. "Your child does not ask of your ability or inability," cosmetics entrepreneur Mary Kay Ash reminds us. "He only asks of your availability." The formula to improving your child's learning is simple: Spend time with your child.

Learning is difficult for many children. It is difficult for parents, as well. For both, learning requires discipline and practice. PASS shows that parents can give their children a head start in school by working with them on forming good study habits at home.

This thrust is in keeping with a proposal by the Carnegie Foundation. It recommended a seven-step approach to improve the educational future of millions of children in America. One step is to launch a mammoth parent-education campaign, with parenting programs in every state, so parents of preschool children can learn how to prepare them for school.

All parents should march in this campaign, especially parents with older children. While many children receive a jump on school through early intervention programs like Head Start and other preschool efforts, recent research shows their benefits are short-lived. They are not enough to survive the rigors of later schooling. Follow-up assistance is necessary. In the end, follow-up programs must be combined with preschool programs to prevent the loss of early learning gains.

Parents are the key to giving children this extra help. If they continue to work with children on study skills and schoolwork throughout their elementary and secondary grades, these children will retain the academic advantages gained during preschool years.

Parenthood is a long, winding trail. Times do get rough along the way. Administering to a child's physical needs takes a lot of sacrifice. Tending to a child's learning needs is even more challenging. It is an area in which most parents have not been trained. Demands on parents are enormous. They are expected to make sure that a child is clothed, fed, and housed. They also are expected to ensure that a child learns. But learning is difficult without good study skills.

Improving a child's study skills is within the reach of all parents. When it comes to their child's school performance, parents need not be helpless like leaves in the wind. They can take control of their children's learning. All they need is the desire to do so, followed by a passionate resolve. Become too lazy about regularly monitoring your children's schoolwork and you cheat them out of an education that is indispensable if they are to have a productive life.

PASS offers many words of advice to parents. None is more moving than that given by a second-grade class in Milwaukee, Wisconsin. This class recites a motto as it begins every school day. This motto can serve as inspiration for parents who love their children and want them to succeed in school.

I know I can.

I know I must.

I know I will.

If it is to be, it's up to me.

If children are the future, parents are the brushes that paint that future. Writer Peter Ustinov characterizes parents in still another way. Parents are the bone on which their children sharpen their teeth.

To build the pathway to excellence in education, parents have to make sure learning happens in the home. Schools can build on that. It is not going to be easy. But it must be done. The more time parents devote to their children's learning at home, the more their children will get out of school.

Learning flourishes when parents do things for their children and invest time in their daily learning. No new study is necessary to show you what has to be done to help underperforming students. The home has to be fueled with high-octane parents. Make the next decade "The Parent Decade in American Education." Do this by taking action now.

What is needed to electrify student learning in America is a massive groundswell of passion for educating children. To truly make a difference, parents must become "crazy" about their children, as suggested by Dr. Urie Bronfenbrenner, a prominent child psychologist. Nothing less than such madness will do.

Today's educators generally single out three problems of children in school: a lack of values, a lack of discipline, and a lack of goals. To this list ought to be added another: a lack of good study habits. Parents can do something about all four. In this manual, they have had the opportunity to concentrate on the last.

If you let your children know that you expect more from them in school, you will soon see the difference. Become a missionary for improving your child's study habits. Start now! Do it! Remember, words will not change things. Action on your part will. Do not give up. Be guided by the slogan: "A winner never quits; a quitter never wins." Raising your child's study skills is the surest way to being a winner in his or her life. Stick with it! Heed the wisdom of Helen Keller: "We can do almost anything we want if we stick with it long enough."

In his 1998 book, *The Discipline of Hope: Learning from a Lifetime of Teaching*, Herbert Kohl insists that all children can learn. Even those who are poor and having a tough time growing up can learn. His "discipline of hope" is that there are absolutely no limits to the potential of a child to be somebody. Learning is a staircase to being somebody for children to climb. And parents should be the chief bodyguard and motivator in their ascent.

Draw energy from the following poem by an unknown author. It describes the way a parent-teacher partnership can unlock the true learning potential of every child.

I dreamed I stood in a studio

And watched two sculptors there,

The clay they used was a young child's mind,

And they fashioned it with care.

One was a teacher; the tools he used

Were books and music and art.

One was a parent with a guiding hand,

And a gentle, loving heart.

Day after day the teacher toiled

With touch that was deft and sure.

While the parent labored by his side

And polished and smoothed it o'er.

And when at last their task was done,

They were proud of what they wrought.

For the things they had molded into the child,

Could neither be sold nor bought.

And each agreed he would have failed

If he had done it alone.

For behind the parent stood the school,

And behind the teacher, the home.

EVALUATION FORM

An evaluation is an exercise used to make a judgment about something's worth. Your opinions are important. Taken together, they enable you to determine the value of your learning experiences.

Please answer the following questions to the best of your ability. The first part deals with personal information. The second part deals with the workbook. Do the best you can in writing responses to each questionnaire item. As mentioned in the beginning of this workbook, tallying and interpreting responses can be done in a peer review session. That is, a group of parents can share, talk about, and go through each question one at a time. Collectively, they can figure out what the responses mean to them. Or a parent can review alone his or her own evaluation form to weigh the workbook's usefulness.

PART 1

1. I am a   ___Female   ___Male

2. My age is   ___19 or under   ___20 to 30   ___40 to 50   ___50+

3. Check which schools your children attend (you can check more than one).
   ___Daycare   ___Elementary   ___Middle School/   ___High School
                                          Junior High
                                          School

4. I live in   ___the city   ___the suburbs   ___a rural area

5. I am a   ___single parent   ___married parent

6. How many children are in your home?_____

PART 2

1. Is the material in this workbook easy to read?
   ___Yes   ___No   ___Undecided

2. Are the chapters (modules) organized in an easy-to-follow way?
   ___Yes   ___No   ___Undecided

3. Which one of the topics below was the most useful for you? Check one.

___Parent Attitude   ___Structuring the Home Environment

___Listening Skills   ___Concentration

___Time Management   ___Homework

___Computers   ___Taking Notes

___Tests   ___Memory Enhancement

___Thinking Skills   ___Reading

4. Which one of the above topics was the least useful?

_____

5. Which topic was the easiest to study?

_____

6. Which topic was the most difficult to study?

_____

7. Which one activity from the menu of activities in the workbook did *your* children like the most? the least?
most_____
least_____

8. Which one activity from the menu of activities in the workbook did *you* like the most? the least?
most_____
least_____

9. Studying this workbook made talking to my children
___easier   ___harder   ___no change

10. Which did you find most effective?
___Working Alone   ___Working With Others

11. Which helpful hints from the workbook have you applied successfully at home to strengthen the study habits of your children? List them below.

_____

_____

12. Which study skills do your children need the most help with? Check more than one if necessary.

___Doing Homework   ___Listening

___Concentrating   ___Managing Time

___Using Computers   ___Preparing for Tests

___Test Taking   ___Memorizing

___Thinking   ___Reading

___Writing   ___Spelling

13. Did the "Study Guide" before each chapter (module) serve as a worthwhile introduction to the chapter with its "Focus, Purpose, Skill, and Reflection" overview?
___Yes   ___No   ___Don't Know

14. Did going over the five major topics on study skills bring back memories of your own school days?
___Yes   ___No   ___Can't Recall

15. When you were in school, did your parents take the time to help you with the study habits covered in this workbook?
___Yes   ___No   ___Can't Recall

16. Could you have done better in school if you had acquired the study habits covered in this workbook?
___Yes   ___No   ___Don't Know

17. Now that you have completed this workbook, do you feel confident in your ability to help your kids strengthen their study skills?
___Yes   ___No   ___Don't Know

18. Upon completion of this workbook, do you feel that you helped other parents do a better job teaching their kids study skills?
___Yes   ___No   ___Don't Know

19. What do you think is the **strongest** feature of this workbook?

_____

_____

20. What do you think is the **weakest** feature of this workbook?

_____

_____

21. What would you do to improve this workbook?

_____

_____

22. In a few words, state your feelings about having completed this workbook and, in a sense, "graduated" from this program.

_____

_____

ABOUT THE AUTHOR

John R. Ban is a professor emeritus of education and was a coordinator of adminstrator programs at Indiana University Northwest in Gary, Indiana. Long active in civic affairs, he has been a president of a school board, chairman of a metropolitan police commission, and a member of many community committees. He has been a public school teacher and university administrator.

Dr. Ban is the author of several books and numerous journal articles on public education. He has worked extensively with teachers, students, and parents. He has also been active in establishing parenting workshops for prison inmates and violence education programs for inner-city parents. Dr. Ban is married and the father of four children.

Make the Most of Your
Professional Development Investment

Let National Educational Service schedule time for you and your staff with leading practitioners in the areas of:

- **Professional Learning Communities** with Richard DuFour, Robert Eaker, Rebecca DuFour, and associates
- **Effective Schools** with associates of Larry Lezotte
- **Assessment for Learning** with Rick Stiggins and associates
- **Crisis Management and Response** with Cheri Lovre
- **Discipline With Dignity** with Richard Curwin and Allen Mendler
- **SMART School Teams** with Jan O'Neill and Anne Conzemius
- **Passport to Success** (parental involvement) with Vickie Burt
- **Peacemakers** (violence prevention) with Jeremy Shapiro

Additional presentations are available in the following areas:

- At-Risk Youth Issues
- Bullying Prevention/Teasing and Harassment
- Team Building and Collaborative Teams
- Data Collection and Analysis
- Embracing Diversity
- Literacy Development
- Motivating Techniques for Staff and Students

national educational service
304 W. Kirkwood Avenue
Bloomington, IN 47404-5132
(812) 336-7700
(800) 733-6786 (toll-free number)
FAX (812) 336-7790

NEED MORE COPIES OR ADDITIONAL RESOURCES ON THIS TOPIC?

Need more copies of this book? Want your own copy? Need additional resources on this topic? If so, you can order additional materials by using this form or by calling us toll free at (800) 733-6786 or (812) 336-7700. Or you can order by FAX at (812) 336-7790.

Title	Price*	Quantity	Total
Parents Assuring Student Success	$ 24.95		
Building Successful Partnerships: A Guide for Developing Parent and Family Involvement Programs	18.95		
How Smart Schools Get and Keep Community Support	24.95		
Professional Learning Communities at Work	24.95		
Professional Learning Communities at Work video	495.00		
Creating Learning Communities	18.95		
Reclaiming Youth at Risk	21.95		
Reclaiming Our Prodigal Sons and Daughters	18.95		
Power Struggles	9.95		
Discipline with Dignity for Challenging Youth	24.95		
What Do I Do When...? How to Achieve Discipline with Dignity	21.95		
Adventure Education for the Classroom Community curriculum	89.00		
		SUBTOTAL	
		SHIPPING	
Please add 6% of order total. For orders outside the continental U.S., please add 8% of order total.			
		HANDLING	
Please add $4. For orders outside the continental U.S., please add $6.			
		TOTAL (U.S. funds)	

*Price subject to change without notice.

❏ Check enclosed   ❏ Purchase order enclosed
❏ Money order   ❏ VISA, MasterCard, Discover, or American Express (circle one)
Credit Card No._____ Exp. Date _____
Cardholder Signature _____

SHIP TO:
First Name_____ Last Name_____
Position _____
Institution Name_____
Address_____
City_____ State_____ ZIP _____
Phone_____ FAX _____
E-mail _____

304 W. Kirkwood Ave.
Bloomington, IN 47404-9107
(812) 336-7700 • (800) 733-6786 (toll-free number)
FAX (812) 336-7790

national educational service